**Pierrick
Picot**

**Producers
Frank Ash
Merilyn Harris**

When in
France

**A HOLIDAYMAKER'S GUIDE
TO THE LANGUAGE AND THE PEOPLE**

BBC BOOKS

This book accompanies the BBC television series
When in France, first broadcast on BBC 2 from
spring 1990 (produced by Frank Ash), and the
radio series of the same name, first broadcast on
Radio 4 from spring 1990 (produced by Merilyn
Harris).

Published to accompany a series of programmes
prepared in consultation with the BBC
Educational Broadcasting Council.

Front cover and inside photographs copyright
Christopher Drew. Front cover shows the
château at Hautefort.

Line illustrations copyright Mike Gilkes.

© Pierrick Picot 1990
First published 1990

Published by BBC Books, a division of BBC
Enterprises Ltd, Woodlands, 80 Wood Lane,
London W12 0TT

ISBN 0 563 21507 0

Set in 9 on 10½ point Century Schoolbook by
Ebenezer Baylis & Son Ltd, Worcester

Printed and bound in Great Britain by
Ebenezer Baylis & Son Ltd, Worcester
Colour separations by
Ebenezer Baylis & Son Ltd, Worcester
Cover printed by Richard Clay Ltd, Norwich

CONTENTS

ABOUT THIS BOOK

● It's for people who are attracted by France and would like to know something about the country, its people and its language. It's also for those who would like to brush up their French.

● It has been written with this in mind so that visitors can make the most of their holiday. It can be followed alongside the BBC tv and radio series *When in France.* It's your survival kit in France!

● It's divided into 15 sections called **unités** (units). Each unit covers a particular theme (food, shopping, travelling, etc.) and comprises 5 parts:

● handy words and expressions/phrases to help you start speaking French,
● two or three short dialogues/conversations where these words and expressions are put into context,
● some simple explanations why in French it is like this and not like that,
● plenty of opportunities to test yourself,
● some useful information about what you may need to know while in France.

● At the back of the book, you'll find a very basic grammar, a glossary of additional words and expressions for each **unité** and a French–English vocabulary. Don't hesitate to look at them as you go along.

HOW TO USE IT

● It's probably best to start with the first **unité**, but you can really use them in any order.

● Start by reading the few notes at the beginning of each **unité**, which set the scene, followed by a few handy words and expressions/phrases.

● Then read **Action** which comprises the dialogues/ conversations. There is a pronunciation guide on pages 7-9 to help you.

- Afterwards carry on with **Replay** which tells you a bit more about how the language works.
- Finally test how much you've learned by answering the **Tryout** and the **Quiz**. You will find that the exercises are at different levels, some are easier than others. They are there to help you make progress and gain confidence. The answers are at the back. You can do these exercises on your own or with somebody else, especially those where you have to play two parts.

'WHEN IN FRANCE' CASSETTE
There is one C90 cassette accompanying this book which will help you get practice in French. On it Polly James learns to use the French from each **unité** with the help of Olivier Pierre.

FRANCE AND THE FRENCH

A FEW FACTS

● France is the largest country of the EEC. It is twice the size of Great Britain and not surprisingly offers a variety of contrasting landscapes and climates, from lazy sunshine in Provence, stunning mountain scenery in the Alps, to the spectacular sands and pine forests of the Atlantic coast.

● The population (les Français) is around 56 million, about the same as Britain, but it is unevenly distributed. Parts of France, like the Massif central, are quite empty whereas others, such as the Mediterranean coast, are very crowded.

● France is divided into Metropolitan France and the overseas territories and departments, known as DOM-TOM (départements d'outre-mer et territoires d'outre-mer). There are 95 départements in metropolitan France (including the island of Corsica) and 4 DOM which are la Guadeloupe, la Martinique, la Guyanne and la Réunion.

THE LANGUAGE

There are about 75 million native speakers of French in the world who can be found in Europe, Africa, South-east Asia and North America.

France is rich in dialects, but standard French is spoken everywhere. There are also other languages in their own right such as Breton and Basque.

LETTERS AND SOUNDS
This is only a rough guide to help you cope with pronunciation. It's very hard to get a good accent from a written page, so the following guide is meant to be used with the cassette. Three important points to remember: some sounds will be totally new; at the end of words **e** is not pronounced, nor are most consonants (tabac, petit, premier, vous parlez, nez, les chambres) but there are some exceptions like parc, cognac, espagnol; unlike English words, there is no main stress on a single syllable, instead all syllables are equally stressed.

1 Consonants
The following sound much the same in French and English:

b (bateau); d (demi); f (femme); k (kilo); l (lit); m (malade); n (neuf); p (pain); s (serveur); t (table); v (vin); z (zèbre).

The following sound slightly different:

c	+ a, o, u or consonant is pronounced like 'c' in 'cat' **café; cognac; cuisine; crevette**
c	+ e or i is pronounced like 's' in 'same' **cinq; cent; c'est**
ç	like 's' in 'same' **garçon**
ch	like 'sh' in 'ship' **chaud; marché**

g	+ a, o, u or consonant is pronounced like 'g' as in 'goat' **galette; baguette; grand**
g	+ e or i is pronounced like 's' in 'pleasure' **gîte; manger**
gn	like 'n' in 'opinion' **champagne; Dordogne**
h	is usually not pronounced **hôtel; homme**
j	like 's' in 'leisure' **je; j'aime**
ph	like the English 'f' **phare**
qu	like 'k' in 'kilo' **quatre**
r	comes from the back of the mouth. Listen carefully to the examples on the tape. **bière; restaurant; mer**
th	the same as a single 't' **thé**
t	followed by '-ion' pronounced 's' **station de métro**
w	sometimes as in 'van' **wagon; wc**

2 Vowels

a 1	short as in 'apple' or 'cat' **addition; mal**
a 2	long as in 'car' **pas; âge**
e 1	is generally similar to 'a' as in 'alive' **le; petit**
e 2	is similar to 'e' as in 'bed' **les; c'est; merci; baguette**
	words ending with er and ez (pronounced like é) **vous habitez; premier**

é	is similar to a shortened 'ay' as in 'day' **vélo; métro**
è, ê	is similar to e 2 **père; vous êtes**
i	is similar to 'ee' as in 'seen' **ici; merci; Brigitte**
o	as in 'odd' **Ecosse**
o	at the end of word or **ô**, is similar to 'o' as in 'oval' **vélo; hôtel**
u	is a very French sound. Listen carefully to the examples on the tape. **du; sur; une**

Nasals

Nasals are vowel sounds followed by an 'n'. Listen carefully to the examples on the tape.

1	**in**	**vin; sapin**
	un	**un; chacun**
	ain	**pain; main**
	ien	**chien; combien**
	ein	**plein**
2	**en**	**en; dent** (but in **ils habitent, ent** is not pronounced)
	an	**dans; blanc**
3	**on**	**mon; bon**

THE FIRST STEPS

Try to become familiar with these words and expressions before moving on to the first **unité:**

Bonjour	Good morning/Hello
Bonsoir	Good evening/Goodbye
Au revoir	Goodbye
Bonne nuit	Good night
Enchanté	Pleased to meet you
Bienvenu (en France)	Welcome (to France)
Monsieur	(Messieurs in the plural) Mr/Sir
Madame	(Mesdames ,, ,, ,,) Mrs
Mademoiselle	(Mesdemoiselles ,,) Miss

When you want to greet a group of people where there are men and women present, you say:

Bonjour Messieurs Dames   Good morning ladies and gentlemen

People will also greet you without adding Monsieur or Madame. They may also reverse the order, saying Monsieur, bonjour.

S'il vous plaît	Please
Merci	} Thank you
Je vous remercie	

To say thank you very much, add **beaucoup; Merci beaucoup**

Je vous en prie	My pleasure
De rien	Don't mention it/It's nothing

HOW TO ASK A QUESTION
There are different ways of asking a question. The simplest way is to state something and to raise the intonation at the end:

Vous parlez français? (Do you speak French?)
Vous habitez Dijon? (Do you live in Dijon?)

Another way is by adding **est-ce que** before the subject:

Est-ce que vous parlez anglais? (Do you speak English?)
Où est-ce que vous habitez? (Where do you live?)

With these two examples, you can go quite a long way. For a more complete picture, see pages 73-4.

And remember, only practice makes perfect. Don't bother about your accent or about your mistakes. They'll love you all the more for that!

If you are interested in taking your French further, there is a complete first-stage language pack available from BBC Books entitled *A Vous La France*. It comprises a book and two cassettes.

GETTING A DRINK

WHEN IN FRANCE . . .

You have just landed in France and one of the first things
you'll probably want to do is have a drink. You'll find that
there are many drinks that you will recognise by their
trade names (Perrier or Orangina for example), but many
more will have unusual names or colours. If you drink at
the terrace of a café or even inside sitting at a table, you
will pay more than if you stand up at the bar. And the tip
(**le pourboire**) is nowadays often included in your bill.
But the tradition is still to leave a little extra on the
table.

● To order a drink, just name it and add 'please':

Un café (a small black coffee), **s'il vous plaît**
Un grand crème (a large coffee with milk)
Un demi or **une pression** (a draught beer)
Un schweppes (a tonic water)

● To ask how much it costs:
C'est combien, s'il vous plaît?

ACTION
You and your family have just come off the ferry and have
stopped at a café for a drink.

Waiter	**Bonjour Messieurs Dames.**
You	**Bonjour Monsieur.**
Waiter	**Vous désirez?**
You	**Un grand crème, un demi et deux schweppes, s'il vous plaît.**

A little later:

Waiter	**Voilà, Messieurs Dames.**
You	**Merci. C'est combien, s'il vous plaît?**
Waiter	**Quarante-six francs, s'il vous plaît.**

You and your friend are at the bar. You order two beers, but without saying clearly that you want draught beer. Look what happens!

You	**Bonjour Madame, deux bières s'il vous plaît.**
Waitress	**Bouteille ou pression?**
You	**Pression s'il vous plaît.**

You've all decided to have an aperitif at the terrace of a café. You and your wife will have a **kir** (white wine and blackcurrant liqueur) and the children a **diabolo-menthe** (mint and lemonade). First you have to attract the waitress's attention.

You	**Mademoiselle, s'il vous plaît?**
Waitress	**Oui, tout de suite, Messieurs Dames . . . Vous désirez?**
You	**Deux kirs et deux diabolos-menthe, s'il vous plaît.**
Waitress	**Bien.**

Before the waitress goes to fetch your drinks, you ask her where the toilets are:

You	**Excusez-moi, où sont les toilettes?**
Waitress	**Là-bas, à droite.**
You	**Merci beaucoup.**
Waitress	**Je vous en prie.**

REPLAY

1 When the waiter comes to you, he will ask you what you want to drink. The waiter may say: **Vous désirez?** or **Qu'est-ce que vous désirez?** You may also hear (in a café or at friends') **Qu'est-ce que vous voulez prendre/boire?** (What will you have? What would you like to drink?)

2 To ask where a place or something is, you simply have to follow the same order as in English: **Où est le café?** or **Où sont les toilettes?**

3 Masculine/Feminine. It is important to know whether the noun is masculine or feminine. If it is masculine, use **le** or **un**, if it is feminine **la** or **une.** When is a noun masculine or feminine? Well, only practice makes perfect!

4 Understanding directions can be a daunting task: **à droite** (on/to your right); **à gauche** (on/to your left); **là-bas** (over there); **ici** (here). You will meet more about directions in the following pages.

TRY OUT

1 You want to order a drink, but the waitress has not spotted you yet. Attract her attention.

2 She is now ready to take your order. You would like two small black coffees and one large white coffee.

3 You have finished your drink. Now you ask how much you owe and at the same time you ask where the toilets are.

4 The waitress has just come to take your order. What does she ask you? You reply: two draught beers, one kir and one drink with mint and lemonade.

QUIZ

1 *Scrambled dialogue.* Can you put this dialogue in the right sequence?

A **Où sont les toilettes?**
B **Deux cafés et un demi, s'il vous plaît.**
C **Bonjour Messieurs Dames.**
D **Qu'est-ce que vous désirez?**
E **Bonjour Monsieur.**
F **Là-bas à gauche.**
G **Je vous en prie.**
H **Merci beaucoup.**

2 *Pairing.* What is the right definition for each drink listed below?

A Demi   1 Limonade + menthe
B Crème   2 Vin blanc + cassis
C Diabolo-menthe   3 Bière à la pression
D Kir   4 Café au lait

3 *Jumbled sentence.* Can you put the three sentences into the right order so that they make sense again?

plaît s'il combien vous c'est
que vous qu'est désirez ce
prie vous en je

WORTH KNOWING

Un demi is not quite a 'half' in the British sense. What you get is a quarter of a litre – a little less than half a pint. A demi is generally lager. There are two main categories of beer: **bière blonde** (lager) and **bière brune** (brown ale). In bars and cafés where they have draught as well as bottled beer, you will always be asked **bouteille ou pression?** if you simply ask for **une bière.**

TRAVELLING BY CAR

WHEN IN FRANCE

Driving in France is very pleasant; for one thing, you'll find very few cars in some parts of the country. If you look on a map you will see, for example, N.138 or D.32. N stands for **Nationale** (A road) and D for **Départementale** (B road). France has over 3000 miles of motorways **(autoroutes)** which are mostly toll roads **(à péage)**. Remember that you only pay the péage when you leave the motorway. The number of a motorway always starts with the letter A, for example A.6 (Paris–Lyon). When you stop for petrol **(essence)**, you'll find that it comes in two grades: **ordinaire** (2-star petrol) and **super** (4-star petrol). You'll also find **essence sans plomb** (unleaded petrol – literally petrol without lead). If you have a diesel engine, you will need **gas-oil** (also spelt **gazole**).

● To get a full tank of 4-star petrol, simply ask for:
Le plein de super, s'il vous plaît.

● You can also ask for a certain amount or a certain price:
Vingt litres d'ordinaire, s'il vous plaît.
Cent francs de gas-oil, s'il vous plaît.

● To ask whether there is a petrol station nearby:
Il y a une station-service près d'ici, s'il vous plaît?

ACTION

You stop at the petrol station to fill up your tank with 4-star petrol.

You	**Le plein s'il vous plaît Monsieur.**
Attendant	**Super ou ordinaire?**
You	**Super, s'il vous plaît.**
Attendant	**Bien Monsieur.**

The tank is full and you ask how much it is.

You	**C'est combien, s'il vous plaît?**
Attendant	**Deux cent vingt francs, Monsieur.**

You are looking for the nearest petrol station to get some unleaded petrol. You stop to ask a passer-by.

You	**Pardon, Madame. Il y a une station-service près d'ici s'il vous plaît?**
Passer-by	**Oui, à trois cents mètres à droite.**
You	**Il y a de l'essence sans plomb dans cette station?**
Passer-by	**Oui, Monsieur.**
You	**Merci beaucoup Madame. Au revoir.**
Passer-by	**Je vous en prie. Au revoir.**

REPLAY

1 You already know how to ask how much it is (see unit 1). However, understanding the price may prove more difficult sometimes. To ask the person to repeat, say **Vous pouvez répéter s'il vous plaît?** or **Comment?**

2 Knowing numbers is essential. To revise or learn numbers, see pages 82-3.

3 To ask where you can have/find/buy something say **Où est-ce que je peux avoir/trouver/acheter ...?**

4 A very useful expression to know is **Il y a** (there is/there are) which does not change whether it is singular or plural.

TRY OUT

1 You pull in at a petrol station to fill up your tank (**réservoir**). You ask the attendant for 150,00 francs worth of 4-star petrol.

2 Then you change your mind and say that you want your tank to be filled up.

3 The attendant says 'two hundred and twenty francs'. But you don't quite get it. Ask him to repeat the price. Now what did he say?

4 You desperately need to get some petrol. Ask where there is a petrol station and also ask whether they serve unleaded petrol.

QUIZ

1 *Location.* Imagine that you are looking for these things. Work out first how you would ask the question and then work out the answer, using the instructions given.

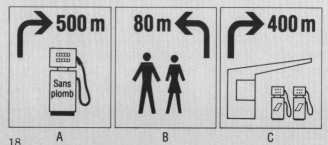

A   B   C

18

2 *The missing line.* You want to find a petrol station where you can get unleaded petrol. You ask a passer-by.

You	(Excuse me, Sir.)
Passer-by	**Oui, Madame.**
You	(Where can I find a petrol station, please?)
Passer-by	**Il y a une station à cent mètres.**
You	(Can you repeat please?)
Passer-by	**A cent mètres.**
You	(Is there unleaded petrol?)
Passer-by	**Oui, Madame.**
You	(Thank you very much.)
Passer-by	**Je vous en prie, Madame.**
You	(Goodbye.)
Passer-by	**Au revoir, Madame.**

3 *Anagrams.* Sort out these anagrams to make words that you have met in this unit.

p e r u s
e r o d a n i r i
l e p i n e l

WORTH KNOWING

If you cannot avoid the major holiday weekends, it is a good idea to follow the advice given on the radio by **Bison Futé** (the cunning buffalo) in order to avoid **les bouchons** (traffic jams) or **les points noirs** (the congested areas). **Bison Futé** will ask you to follow **les Itinéraires Bis** (alternative routes), indicated by green arrows, and **les Itinéraires de délestage** (relief routes) by yellow arrows. Free **Bison Futé** maps are available from petrol stations and motorway toll booths. You will also find that advice is given in English at specific times of the day on the main radio stations.

CHECKING INTO A HOTEL

WHEN IN FRANCE . . .
You'll find many hotels, from the simplest ungraded
hotel to the most luxurious. Hotels are graded from one to
five. If you want to stay several days in the same hotel,
you may be able to choose the full-board (**pension**) or
half-board (**demi-pension**) option. The success of B&B
has also reached France now. You'll see it advertised as
Chambre d'hôte. If they also offer an evening meal, it
will be indicated by **Table d'hôte.**

● To ask whether there is a room free:
Vous avez une chambre de libre?

● With a double bed/a single bed
Avec un grand lit/un lit à une personne.

● With bathroom/shower
Avec salle de bains/douche.

● To say that you have a reservation
J'ai une réservation.

● To give your name
Je m'appelle . . .

ACTION
After a long journey, you arrive at your hotel. You have
already made a reservation.

Receptionist	**Bonsoir Messieurs Dames.**
You	**Bonsoir Madame. J'ai une réservation. Je m'appelle . . .**
Receptionist	**Ah oui! Vous avez réservé deux chambres. C'est pour combien de nuits?**
You	**Pour une nuit.**
Receptionist	**D'accord.**

The following evening, you discover your ideal hotel. But
first, you have to find out if they have two rooms
available.

You	**Bonsoir Madame. Vous avez des chambres de libre, s'il vous plaît?**
Receptionist	**Oui, Monsieur.**
You	**Vous avez une chambre avec un grand lit et une chambre à deux lits?**
Receptionist	**Oui. Avec salle de bains?**
You	**Oui, s'il vous plaît.**

Now you ask how much the room is and whether breakfast is included in the price.

You	**Et c'est combien la chambre?**
Receptionist	**Alors, c'est deux cent cinquante francs la chambre.**
You	**Très bien. Et le petit déjeuner est compris?**
Receptionist	**Ah non, c'est en plus. C'est trente francs le petit déjeuner.**

REPLAY
1 If you have made a reservation, the receptionist will ask your name to check. You will be asked **Votre nom, s'il vous plaît?** or **Comment est-ce que vous vous appelez?**
2 It is worth checking whether breakfast is included in the price of the room. **Le petit déjeuner est compris?** Usually hotels have a price list, often displayed on your bedroom door. Listen out for the expressions **compris** (included) and **en plus** or **en supplément** (extra) in hotels.
3 If you want to ask the receptionist the sort of rooms which are available, say **Qu'est-ce que vous avez comme chambre de libre?** Likewise, the receptionist may ask you the sort of rooms that you would like, **Qu'est-ce que vous voulez comme chambre?**
4 The main meals in France are **le petit déjeuner** (breakfast), **le déjeuner** (lunch), and **le dîner** (evening meal). There is also **le goûter** (afternoon snack) for children.

TRY OUT

1 You and your partner arrive at your hotel. Say that you have made a reservation and give your full name.

2 You're desperately looking for a room. Ask the receptionist whether she has a room free. You're in luck! Tell her that you want a room with shower for three nights.

3 You would like to make a reservation for two bedrooms, one with a double bed and the other one with two single beds. How would you say this? Also ask how much are the bedrooms.

4 Ask whether you can telephone Paris and where the telephone is.

QUIZ

1 *Question and answers.* Match the questions with the answers:

A	**Pour combien de nuits?**	1	**C'est ici à droite**
B	**Le petit déjeuner est compris?**	2	**Une chambre avec un grand lit**
C	**Qu'est-ce que vous voulez comme chambre?**	3	**Cinq nuits**
D	**Où est le téléphone?**	4	**C'est en plus**

2 *Numbers.* Can you say these numbers in French? Try to write them down too.

Le petit déjeuner est 34,00 francs.
La chambre avec douche est 180,00 francs.
La chambre avec salle de bains est 360,00 francs.
Vous avez la chambre numéro 22.

3 *Missing words.* Find the words which have disappeared from this dialogue. To help you each dash represents a letter.

- - - - - - - **Monsieur.**
Bonsoir, Madame, - '- - une réservation. - -
- '- - - - - - - Oliver Cromwell.
- - - - - - - ?
Oliver Cromwell.
Vous avez réservé pour combien de - - - - - ?
- - - - une - - - - .
Une - - - - - - - avec douche?

22

Non. Avec salle de ------.
(It suddenly dawns on you that you are in the wrong hotel)
Mais je suis bien à l'------ de France?
Non, Monsieur, - '---- l'hôtel de Normandie ici.

4 *Pairs.* Match the meals with the time of day.

A **le matin**   1 **le goûter**
B **le midi**   2 **le dîner**
C **l'après-midi**   3 **le déjeuner**
D **le soir**   4 **le petit déjeuner**

WORTH KNOWING

Making a telephone call. The French telecom system is now divided into two main regions, Paris (and its suburbs) and the rest of France **(la province).** All subscribers have an eight-figure number. Here is the way to dial depending on where you are.

1 For calls within France:
Within Paris or within **la province**, dial the eight-figure number only.
From Paris to **la province**, dial 16, wait for the tone, then dial the eight-figure number.
From **la province** to Paris, dial 16 + 1, then the eight-figure number.

2 For international calls:
From France to the UK, first dial 19, wait for the continuous tone, then 44 followed by your STD code minus the first 0, and your number.
From the UK to France, dial 010 33 and then the eight-figure number (for Paris add 1 before the eight-figure number).

Remember that you can phone the UK at a cheap rate (with 50% extra time) between 9.30 pm and 8.00 am every weekday, after 2 pm on Saturdays and all day Sundays. It may also be worth buying **'une télécarte'** (phonecard), from Post Offices for example, which will cost you 40 francs minimum. Phone boxes **(cabines téléphoniques)** receive incoming calls where the blue bell-sign is shown.

SIGHTSEEING

WHEN IN FRANCE

Apart from the many travel guides, the best place to find information about sightseeing is **le syndicat d'initiative** (tourist information office), also called **office de tourisme** or **maison du tourisme**, where you will be able to get **un plan de la ville** (a map of the town) or **une carte de la région** (map of the area).

- To ask where the museum is
Pour aller au musée, s'il vous plaît?

- More directions
Allez tout droit (Go straight on)
C'est en face de (It's in front of)
tout près d'ici (very close by)
à côté de (next to)
au bout de (at the end of)

- Asking for the opening/closing time of the museum
A quelle heure ouvre/ferme le musée, s'il vous plaît?

- Asking for the departure time of the river boat
A quelle heure est le départ du bateau-mouche?

La Pyramide du Louvre, Paris.

ACTION

You are now in Paris and you want to go and browse around the Latin quarter. You ask a passer-by for the direction.

You	**Pardon Monsieur. Pour aller au quartier latin, s'il vous plaît?**
Passer-by	**C'est tout droit, puis la première rue à gauche. Et vous êtes dans le quartier latin.**
You	**Je vous remercie beaucoup.**
Passer-by	**Je vous en prie.**

You want to go to the Musée d'Orsay which is close to your hotel. You ask the receptionist for the way and the opening time.

You	**Excusez-moi, Mademoiselle. Où est le Musée d'Orsay, s'il vous plaît?**
Receptionist	**C'est tout près d'ici. Vous tournez à droite à la sortie de l'hôtel. Puis tout droit, et la troisième rue à gauche. C'est au bout de la rue.**
You	**D'accord. Et à quelle heure ouvre le musée?**
Receptionist	**Il ouvre à 9 heures 30.**
You	**Merci beaucoup Mademoiselle. Au revoir.**
Receptionist	**Au revoir Madame et bonne journée.**

You are planning a trip on the river Seine in a river boat (**bateau-mouche**). You enquire about the departure times (**heures des départs**) and the cost.

You	**Excusez-moi Madame. A quelle heure est le départ du bateau-mouche?**
Woman	**Il y a un départ toutes les heures. Le premier bateau est à 10 heures.**
You	**Et c'est combien?**
Woman	**Alors c'est trente francs pour les adultes et dix francs pour les enfants.**

REPLAY

1 First, Second, Third . . . **Premier, Deuxième, Troisième.** They are called ordinal numbers. To form them, just add 'ième' to the number: for example, **deux** changes into **deuxième**; **trois** into **troisième**, etc. **Un** is the only real exception. It changes completely to become **premier** or **première**. Also when the number ends with an e, it drops this e, for instance **douze . . . douzième** (see pages 82–3 for a list of these numbers).

2 Masculine/Feminine. You have already noticed **le premier bateau** (masculine) and **la première rue** (feminine). Remember that words which accompany the noun have to agree with it. Example: **un grand crème, une grande chambre.**

3 There is a departure every hour: **Il y a un départ toutes les heures.** Every quarter of an hour and every half-hour are **tous les quarts d'heure** and **toutes les demi-heures**. And if it is every 10 (20) minutes, say **toutes les dix (vingt) minutes.**

4 To tell the time, start with **Il est**. For example, **Il est dix heures** (it is 10 o'clock). **Il est dix heures et demie** (it is half-past ten). **Il est 11 heures moins le quart** (it is a quarter to eleven). But note midday is **midi** and midnight is **minuit**. A.M. is **du matin** and P.M. is **de l'après-midi** (until 6.00) and **du soir** (after 6.00). To ask the time, say **Quelle heure est-il, s'il vous plaît?**

5 When **de** is followed by **le** (i.e. 'of the'), it has to change and becomes **du**, as in **le départ du bateau-mouche. De la, de l'** or **des** (**de + les**) also mean 'of the'. (For more information, see page 72.)

TRY OUT

1 A passer-by has just asked you where the Latin quarter is. What did she say? Now tell her it's straight on, then the first street on her left and the second on her right. Add that it is close by.

2 Ask the receptionist in your hotel what time it is and then ask her the opening time of the museum.

3 The receptionist says that it is 9.30 and that the museum opens at 10 o'clock. But you did not quite get it. Ask her to repeat. Got it now? So what's the opening time?

QUIZ

1 *Numbers.* Try to find the ordinal numbers.

Un
Quatre
Onze
Vingt
Vingt-deux

2 *Time is up.* Can you tell the time from the clocks below?

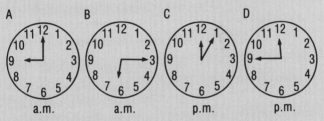

A   B   C   D

a.m.   a.m.   p.m.   p.m.

3 *Orienteering.* Indicate the way to go to **les Halles** in Paris.

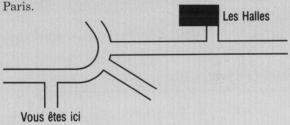

Les Halles

Vous êtes ici

WORTH KNOWING

In Paris, you will find computerised travel information points on the pavement, called **Situ**. **Situ** is designed to help you find the quickest or the shortest way to travel in Paris 'intra muros'. You key in the address you want and you get a small print-out telling you the best métro line to use for example and how long it will take you to reach your destination. It is also worth knowing that parking is free in Paris in August.

To visit national and municipal Museums in Paris, you can buy a 3- or 5-day pass called **La Carte** which entitles you to free admission to 60 museums and monuments.

27

SHOPPING FOR CLOTHES

WHEN IN FRANCE . . .

If you have a free afternoon in town, you may want to go window-shopping (**faire du lèche-vitrines – lécher** means to lick). Spot the **Soldes** sign for a bargain. To know the most fashionable streets (**les rues à la mode**), it is worth asking at the tourist office. Shopping is also a very good way to test yourself. Here are a few expressions worth knowing.

● If you want to try on a skirt/pair of trousers, for example:

Je peux essayer cette jupe/ce pantalon s'il vous plaît?

● Size is always a problem. The shop assistant will ask what size you are.

Quelle est votre taille?

● Just answer by giving your size or you may hear people say, for example:

Je fais du trente-huit.

● It's too small, too big, too long, too short.

C'est trop petit, trop grand, trop long, trop court.

ACTION

You've found a skirt that you like. You try it on.

You	**Je peux essayer cette jupe s'il vous plaît?**
Shop assistant	**Oui bien sûr.**

You like it very much but it is not the right size.

You	**C'est trop petit.**
Shop assistant	**Quelle est votre taille?**
You	**Je fais du quarante-deux.**
Shop assistant	**Ah! Je n'ai pas votre taille. Je suis désolée, Madame.**

You want to buy a pair of swimming trunks for your son.

You	**Vous avez des maillots de bain, s'il vous plaît?**
Shop assistant	**Oui, Madame. Quelle taille?**
You	**C'est pour mon fils. Vingt-quatre.**
Shop assistant	**Quelle couleur?**
You	**Bleu.**
Shop assistant	**Voilà, Madame.**
You	**Très bien. C'est combien?**
Shop assistant	**Soixante-cinq francs, s'il vous plaît.**

REPLAY

1 My . . . Your. My can be **mon** or **ma** (depending whether the word that follows is masculine or feminine). But note that a feminine word starting with a vowel will use **mon**, for example **mon assiette** (my plate). It changes to **mes** in the plural. Your is either **votre** in the singular or **vos** in the plural.

2 Knowing how to apologise is absolutely essential. You already know **Excusez-moi** and you have just learned **Je suis désolé(e)**. Here is another one: **Pardon**.

3 If you want to say that your trousers are far too big or a bit too small, you can use the following: too **(trop)**, far too much **(beaucoup trop)**, a little **(un peu)**, very **(très)**.

4 To turn a sentence into a negative, you have to place on each side of the verb two little words **ne . . . pas**. Here are two examples: **Je ne comprends pas** (I don't understand) or **Ce n'est pas trop petit** (It's not too small). Note that the **ne** becomes **n'** if the verb starts with a vowel or an h which is not pronounced **(je n'habite pas à Paris)**.

TRY OUT

1 Tell the shop assistant that you want a skirt and what your size is. (There is a table giving continental sizes on page 77.)

2 Ask the shop assistant whether you can try this pair of trousers. Say that they are much too long.

3 You've just tried two pairs of trousers. The first one is too small and the second one is too big. How would you say this to the shop assistant? (Remember how to say first, second?) She needs to know your size. How would she ask you? And what would you answer?

QUIZ

1 *Sizes.* Using **un peu, beaucoup trop, trop** and the adjective **grand**, make four possible sentences, starting with **Mon pantalon est . . .** Then try with **Ma jupe est . . .**

2 *Shapes.* How would you describe the following figures, using these adjectives: **petit, grand, gros** (big) and **mince** (thin). You may need to use two together.

3 *Letter-jam.* Can you disentangle the question below?
jupepeuxcettes'ilvousplaîtjeessayer?

4 *Negatives.* Put the following sentences into the
negative:

Je parle français
C'est trop grand
Je suis anglais
Je m'appelle Edward

WORTH KNOWING

Shops are open at least until 6 and often later. Smaller
shops tend to shut between 12 and 2, but some reopen
even later. In general, hypermarkets stay open till 9 or 10
at night. Many shops close all or half-day Monday.

Buying is one thing, paying is another when you are not
familiar with the currency. The Franc (F) is divided into
100 centimes (c). There are coins for 5c, 10c, 20c, ½F, 2F,
5F, 10F and 100F (a new white and gold 10F was
introduced in 1988). There are notes for 20F, 50F, 100F,
200F and 500F. You will see that nowadays the centimes
are rounded off to the nearest decimal. In supermarkets,
for example, if your bill comes up to 20F22, you will only
pay 20F20.

EATING OUT

WHEN IN FRANCE . . .

Outside restaurants you will usually see two or three set menus displayed and an **'A la carte'** list. Usually there will be a **'plat du jour'** (dish of the day) and a **menu gastronomique** (often the top-priced menu with specialities of the region).

● To ask for a table:

Une table pour quatre, s'il vous plaît.

● To order your choice of food:

Deux menus à cinquante-huit (francs), s'il vous plaît.

● To order drinks with the meal:

Une bouteille de vin blanc de pays.
Une bouteille d'eau minérale.

● And finally, to ask for the bill:

L'addition s'il vous plaît.

ACTION

You and your family have finally chosen your menu. Your children will have the **'menu à 58,00 francs'** and you and your wife the **'menu gastronomique'**.

Waiter	**Vous avez choisi?**
You	**Oui, deux menus à cinquante-huit pour les enfants et deux menus gastronomiques, s'il vous plaît.**
Waiter	**Et comme boisson?**
You	**Une bouteille de vin blanc.**
Waiter	**Qu'est-ce que vous voulez comme vin blanc?**
You	**Un vin blanc de pays s'il vous plaît, et aussi une bouteille d'eau minérale.**
Waiter	**Merci.**

You have finished your meal. You call the waiter.

You	**Monsieur, s'il vous plaît . . . l'addition.**
Waiter	**Oui Monsieur, tout de suite.**

You are in a hurry and want to have a quick meal. You order the dish of the day and a bottle of mineral water.

Waiter	**Bonjour, Madame.**
You	**Bonjour, Monsieur.**

(leading you to a table)

Waiter	**Par ici, s'il vous plaît . . . Qu'est-ce que vous désirez?**
You	**Le plat du jour s'il vous plaît et une bouteille d'eau minérale.**
Waiter	**Très bien, Madame.**

REPLAY

1 The waiter will give you the menu and then ask you a bit later on whether you are ready to order: **Vous avez choisi? Vous avez décidé?**

2 To order one of the set menus, you just have to specify its price: **Le menu à 75,00.**

3 One of the ways to ask for (more) bread or more wine is to say **Je peux avoir du pain/une autre bouteille de vin?**

4 When the waitress comes to take your order, she will ask you which wine/starter/main dish you want. **Qu'est-ce vous voulez comme boisson/hors-d'oeuvre/plat principal?** Or she may ask what you would like to start with/follow with: **Pour commencer?/ et ensuite?**

5 Of is translated by **de**. For example, 'a cup of coffee' (**une tasse de café**), 'a bottle of mineral water' (**une bouteille d'eau minérale**). Note that **de** becomes **d'** before a word starting with a vowel or an h which is not pronounced (**chambre d'hôte**).

TRY OUT

1 You and your friend have decided to go and eat out. You ask for a table for two, for the menu with the specialities of the region, and a bottle of red wine.

2 You are cycling and just want to stop for a quick lunch. You decide to have the dish of the day and ice cream (**une glace**) as a dessert, with a bottle of mineral water.

3 You are at the restaurant and have finished your meal. But the waiter seems to have forgotten you. Call him and ask for two coffees and the bill.

4 Ask for a set menu at 65,00 francs and a bottle of white wine from the area.

QUIZ

1 *Gap filling.* Can you find the missing word in each sentence? The dashes will help you (one per letter).

Vous - - - - choisi?
Une bouteille de vin rouge, s'il vous - - - - - ?
Le - - - - à soixante-cinq.
S'il vous plaît, - '- - - - - - - - -.
Une bouteille d'- - - - - - - - - - - -.

2 *What was the question?* Here are the answers to the waiter's questions. What was it the waiter asked in each case? You can suggest more than one question for each answer.

34

Trois menus à cent dix francs.
Une salade de tomates.
Une bouteille de vin rouge de pays.

3 *Pairs.* Find a word from the right-hand column which pairs with one in the left-hand column.

A	**Salé**	1	**Froid**
B	**Saignant**	2	**Cuit**
C	**Chaud**	3	**A point**
D	**Cru**	4	**Sucré**

4 *Specialities.* Match the following specialities with their town or region:

A	**Cassoulet**	1	**Bretagne**
B	**Crêpes**	2	**Bourgogne**
C	**Coq au vin**	3	**Toulouse**
D	**Bouillabaisse**	4	**Alsace**
E	**Choucroute**	5	**Marseille**

WORTH KNOWING

The idea of a 'set meal' is very widespread in French restaurants, from the simplest to the most luxurious. Restaurants will frequently offer several menus by price. You simply choose from the list of **hors-d'oeuvre, plat principal** (main course) and desserts. Usually the higher the price, the wider the choice and, sometimes, the number of courses (like a separate fish course). Sometimes you'll have to choose between **dessert** and **fromage** (cheese). Look out for the words **boisson comprise** (drink included in the price) and **boisson en supplément** or **en sus** (extra). If the drinks are included, you'll get a quarter litre of local wine **(vin de pays)** served in a **carafe** or in a **pichet** (jug) or a small mineral water. If the drinks are extra, it's worth trying **la réserve du patron** (house wine) which is generally very good value. If you decide to choose your meal from the menu **(à la carte)**, then you'll pay quite a lot more for it.

TRAVELLING BY RAIL

WHEN IN FRANCE

If you decide to travel by rail, you'll find the French railway service fast and comfortable. There are many ways of travelling at discounted fares (**tickets à prix réduits**) such as the France Vacances Pass which offers unlimited mileage throughout France on any four days within a fortnight or any nine days within a month. If you are under twenty-six you need pay only 50% of the fare if you have **le Carré Jeune** or **la Carte Jeune**. On some trains children are well catered for, with crêche or playroom facilities. Also at many stations you'll be able to hire bikes.

● To ask for a single or a return:
Un aller simple.
Un aller-retour.

● First class or second class:
En première classe or just **en première**.
En deuxième classe or **en seconde**.

● To ask if there is a train to . . .
Il y a un train pour . . .?

● To ask at what time the train leaves or arrives:
A quelle heure part/arrive le train?

ACTION

You're leaving Paris and are off to Vannes. Your train leaves from Montparnasse railway station, but first you have to take the **métro** to get there. You ask for help to go from Les Tuileries métro station to Montparnasse.

You	**Un ticket, s'il vous plaît?**
Clerk	**Voilà, cinq francs.**
You	**Pour aller à la gare Montparnasse, s'il vous plaît?**
Clerk	**C'est la direction 'Neuilly'. Vous changez à 'Concorde'. Puis direction 'Mairie d'Issy'.**

Métro station in Paris.

(There is more information about the métro in Worth Knowing, page 39.)

You've arrived at Montparnasse station. You're enquiring about trains to Vannes. Time is running short to catch the first one. What about the next one?

You	**Il y a un train pour Vannes?**
Clerk	**Oui. Vous avez un train à neuf heures quatorze. Il part dans deux minutes.**
You	**Et le suivant est à quelle heure?**
Clerk	**Il est à onze heures trente-six. Et il arrive à quinze heures cinquante-cinq.**

You buy a second-class return ticket to Vannes and ask which platform (**quai**) to go to.

You	**Un aller-retour en seconde pour Vannes, s'il vous plaît.**
Clerk	**Voilà. Trois cent cinquante francs.**
You	**C'est quel quai?**
Clerk	**Quai numéro cinq.**
You	**Je vous remercie.**
Clerk	**Je vous en prie.**

REPLAY
1 To specify a particular train, people may say: **le prochain train** (the next train), **le train suivant** (the one after that), **le train de 9h28** (the 9.28 train), **le Paris–Brest** (the train going from Paris to Brest; it is also the name of a cake).

2 To ask whether a seat is free or taken, ask **C'est libre?** or **C'est occupé?**

3 A train timetable is **un horaire des trains.** To be able to read a timetable, you will need to know some of the terms used, such as **circule** (runs), **tlj = tous les jours** (every day), **sauf** (except), **à partir de** (from), **jusqu'au** (till). Example: **circule tous les jours à partir du 25/09 jusqu'au 22/05 sauf les dimanches.**

4 To ask which platform a train leaves from, say **Le train pour Paris part de quel quai?** (you will also see or hear the word **voie** for **quai**). To ask for the left luggage office, **Où est la consigne?**

5 Which train? What time? What in this case is **Quel/Quelle**. It can be preceded by other words such as **A quelle heure** (at what time) or **Sur quel quai** (on which platform).

TRY OUT

1 Ask for two second-class return tickets to Lyons and which platform the train leaves from.

2 You've missed your train. Ask the inspector what time the next train is. Also enquire about its time of arrival.

3 The inspector says that there is a train at 21.15. Find two ways of saying this time.

4 You're at a métro station. Ask a woman nearby how to get to the Gare du Nord. She tells you to take the Porte de Clignancourt direction. How does she say this?

QUIZ

1 *Muddled sentence.* Can you reorganise the two sentences so that you can get the right information?

a **train tous circule dimanches les sauf jours les le**

b **à 7h08 il d'Angers arrive à Nantes part et à 8h13**

2 *Signs.* Can you change these English signs into French?

A　　　　　　　　　　　B

C [PLATFORM]   D [UNDERGROUND]

3 *Time.* Can you translate the following times into words? There are at least two ways of saying them each time.

17.08
23.47
 0.24

WORTH KNOWING

The state-owned SNCF (**Société Nationale des Chemins de Fer Français**) offers an extensive rail network, one of the largest in Europe. The TGV (**train à grande vitesse** or high speed train) is the showpiece of the French railway, going to more than thirty-six cities throughout France. You need to reserve seats on the TGV. The Corail service is also very fast and comfortable. At the station, remember that you must validate (**composter**) your ticket in one of the orange machines at the entrance to the platforms. It is also always worth checking that there are no extra charges you need to pay for the particular train you want to catch, otherwise you might be fined!

The Paris **métro** (the tube) is fast and modern. You can buy tickets individually or by the book (**un carnet de dix tickets**), which is much cheaper. It may also be worth getting a **carte orange** which is a weekly (**hebdomadaire**) or monthly (**mensuel**) card. When you buy a ticket, you don't need to give your destination unless you travel out of Paris by the RER. The RER lines (**Réseau Express Régional**) provide a very fast service to get across Paris or out to the suburbs. Métro lines have no names as in London, but they each have a number which you can use to identify the line you want. Generally speaking, people choose their line by looking at the last station of the line. If you need to change lines during your journey, follow the signs **Correspondances**. They always give the name of the end-of-the-line station.

RENTING A GÎTE

WHEN IN FRANCE

For a quiet holiday, the **gîte** can be an ideal solution.
Gîtes are self-catering accommodation situated
predominantly in rural France. A **gîte** may be a small
cottage, a village house, a flat or a part of a farm. **Gîtes**
are graded by ears of corn from one to three. The owner
(**le propriétaire**) or a neighbour (**un voisin**) will in most
cases be there to welcome you on your arrival. They will
show you round the house and help you with your
immediate needs. You may also be able to buy **les
produits de la ferme** (local farm produce) such as milk,
butter, vegetables, meat. There are also **gîtes d'étapes**
which are night stop-overs for hikers or long-distance
cyclists for example.

● To ask somebody for the keys:
Vous avez les clés?

● To ask where you turn on/off the electricity, the water
or the gas (at the mains):
Pour ouvrir (or **mettre**)/**fermer** (or **couper**)
l'électricité, l'eau, le gaz?

● To say that the cooker does not work:
La cuisinière ne marche pas.

● To say that there is a leak:
Il y a une fuite.

ACTION

You've arrived at your **gîte**. First you go and get the keys
from a neighbour.

You	**Bonjour Madame.**
Neighbour	**Bonjour Monsieur.**
You	**Je m'appelle . . .**
Neighbour	**Ah oui. C'est la famille anglaise.**
You	**Oui. Est-ce que je peux avoir les clés, s'il vous plaît.**
Neighbour	**Oui, bien sûr.**

The neighbour accompanies you to the **gîte** to show you round. You ask where to turn on the gas.

Neighbour	**Voici la cuisine . . . Et voilà le salon.**
You	**Très bien. C'est grand . . . Et pour ouvrir le gaz s'il vous plaît, c'est où?**
Neighbour	**C'est ici.**
You	**D'accord.**

You also ask the neighbour where the beach is and whether there is a supermarket nearby.

You	**Où est la plage s'il vous plaît?**
Neighbour	**C'est à trois kilomètres d'ici.**
You	**Et il y a un supermarché près d'ici?**
Neighbour	**Oui, c'est à dix minutes en voiture.**

Two days later, you go and see the neighbour to tell her that the cooker does not work and that there is a water leak in the bathroom.

You	**Bonjour Madame. La cuisinière ne marche pas.**
Neighbour	**Ah bon?**
You	**Et il y a aussi une fuite d'eau dans la salle de bains.**
Neighbour	**Bon! J'arrive dans cinq minutes.**

REPLAY

1 'We' is **nous**. The ending of the verb changes as with **je** and **vous**. With **nous**, the verb ends with **ons** as a general rule, the exception being **nous sommes** (we are).

2 'Here is the kitchen'. To express 'here' and 'there', use **voici** and **voilà**. Compare **Voici le salon** and **Le voici**, which translate 'Here is the sitting-room' and 'Here it is' ('it' referring to the sitting-room). 'There are the keys' would be **Voilà les clés** and 'There they are' would be **Les voilà**.

3 For a list of the different rooms of the house, see page 79.

4 To express duration, here are a few useful expressions of time: a week (**une semaine**), a fortnight (**quinze jours** or **une quinzaine**), a month (**un mois**). Example: **J'ai loué un gîte pour un mois**.

TRY OUT

1 You're describing your **gîte** to a friend. Tell her that it has three bedrooms, a large sitting-room and a small kitchen and a very big garden.

2 How would you say: 'Here is the bathroom', 'There is the kitchen' and 'There she is'?

3 You enquire about how to turn on the electricity and the water. What do you say?

4 You meet some people in a restaurant and you ask them whether they are staying in a hotel. They reply that they have a **gîte**. Ask them how long they are here for. They say six weeks. Can you make up the dialogue?

QUIZ

1 *Lost property.* Can you answer the questions using the prompt between brackets?

Où sont les clés?	(There they are)
Où sont vos enfants?	(Here they are)
Où est ma femme?	(There she is)
Où est le gîte	(There it is)

2 *We plus verb ending.* Can you answer each question starting with Oui, nous . . . and then with Non, nous . . . (see page 30 (**unité 5**) to revise how to turn a sentence into the negative).

Vous parlez français?
Vous habitez au Pays de Galles?
Vous êtes écossais?

3 *Bad line.* You've been sent a fax confirming the booking of your **gîte**. But part of the message has got muddled up.

Je confirme . . . du réservation gîte un mois Pézenas la pour à

WORTH KNOWING

Something may go wrong in your **gîte**, such as a leaking tap, or the electricity may cut out. Here are a few words and phrases to cope with the imponderables of life:

une coupure de courant – a power cut
un disjoncteur – a circuit-breaker
un fusible – a fuse
les plombs ont sauté – the fuses have gone
une ampoule – a bulb
une prise – a plug, a socket
une prise pour rasoir électrique – a razor point
une prise multiple – an adaptor
un interrupteur – a switch
un compteur – meter
allumer – to switch on
éteindre – to switch off
le robinet fuit – the tap is leaking
une fuite de gaz – a gas leak
le chauffage central – the central heating
le radiateur électrique est en panne – the electric radiator does not work

BREAKING THE ICE

WHEN IN FRANCE . . .

People in France greet each other not only with words but they also shake hands every time they meet. The handshake (**la poignée de main**) is an automatic gesture and people are surprised if you just stand there without offering your hand. Young people tend to kiss each other on the cheeks two or even three times. People still remain fairly formal when they address each other. The first name is not used often as in Britain when you don't know the person well. Even at work, people may still call each other **Monsieur/Madame/Mademoiselle** followed by their surname.

● To say your nationality:
Je suis anglais(e), écossais(e), gallois(e), irlandais(e).

● To say which country or town you live in:
For a country, it's

	en Irlande.
J'habite	**en Angleterre.**
	en Ecosse.
But	**au Pays de Galles.**

For a town, it's

	à Cardiff.
J'habite	**à Manchester.**
	à Dundee.

● To say where you come from:
Je suis de Bristol.

● To ask 'How are you?'
Comment allez-vous?

ACTION
You meet an anglophile who is very inquisitive.

Man	**Comment est-ce que vous vous appelez?**
You	**Je m'appelle Thomas.**
Man	**Vous êtes anglais?**
You	**Non, je suis gallois.**
Man	**Vous habitez à Cardiff?**
You	**Non, j'habite à Edimbourg.**

The owner of your **gîte** would like to know more about you.

Owner	**Bonjour Monsieur. Comment allez-vous?**
You	**Très bien merci. Et vous?**
Owner	**Ça va. Où est-ce que vous habitez en Angleterre?**
You	**J'habite à Chichester.**
Owner	**C'est où exactement?**
You	**C'est près de Portsmouth.**

REPLAY

1 'You' can be **vous** or **tu**. As a general rule, it is best to use **vous**. If the people you are with address you as **tu**, then you can start using it too, but wait for the French to give you the lead. That way, you won't offend anyone by being too familiar. The only time you would use **tu** immediately is when you are talking to young children – for instance, **Comment t'appelles-tu?**

2 How are you? You will hear people say: **Vous allez bien?** or **Comment ça va?** or just **Ça va?** You can reply by saying **Je vais bien, merci** or **Ça va, merci**. If you don't feel well, use the negative: **Je ne vais pas bien** or **Ça ne va pas**. You will hear people say **Ça va pas** without the **ne**.

3 When you want to know where somebody comes from, you can also say: **Vous êtes d'où?** or **Vous êtes d'ici?**

TRY OUT

1 Say that you are English from London, but live in Scotland.

2 How would you ask a child her name? How would you ask an adult?

3 You suspect the waiter is not French. Ask him where he is from. He tells you he comes from Madrid.

4 Introduce yourself: name, nationality and address.

QUIZ

1 *Loss of identity.* Fill in the missing words.

Je - '- - - - - - Barbara. J' - - - - - - à Londres. Je - - suis - - - française. Je - - - - anglaise.

2 *Jumbled dialogues.* Put this dialogue in the correct order.

A **A Londres?**
B **Vous habitez en France?**
C **Je m'appelle Thomas.**
D **Non à Bristol.**
E **Comment est-ce que vous vous appelez?**
F **Non, j'habite en Angleterre.**

3 *Letter removal.* Remove some of the letters to find out the three hidden nationalities.

SFSRASNSCAIS
NANGNLANIS
CECCOSCSACIS

WORTH KNOWING

Number plates (**plaques d'immatriculation**)
French number plates can tell you which part of France people come from. The last two digits indicate the **département** where the car is registered. Incidentally, by law you must change your number plate when you move your main home to another **département**. A few examples of **département** numbers: 33 (Gironde); 75 (Paris); 68 (Haut-Rhin); 83 (Var).

'Name plates'
In France, people are referred to by the town they come from. For example, if you are from Lyons, you are a Lyonnais or a Lyonnaise. You'll find many of these words crop up in French cuisine too. Here are a few examples, some obvious, others less so:

Paris	**Parisien(ne)**
Nantes	**Nantais(e)**
Bourgogne	**Bourguignon(ne)**
Châteaubriand	**Castelbriantais(e)**
Provence	**Provençal(e)**
Saint Etienne	**Stéphanois(e)**
Tours	**Tourangeau/Tourangelle**

SHOPPING FOR FOOD

WHEN IN FRANCE . . .
Shopping for food is a serious business. Local markets,
whether they be fruit and vegetables (**fruits et légumes**),
meat (**viande**) and fish (**poissons**), are often the best
place to do your shopping in terms of freshness and
quality. You'll have to use the word **un kilo** or **une livre**
or give the number of grammes. A kilo is just over two
pounds. Half a kilo is **une livre** and a quarter of a kilo
une demi-livre. If you want to buy three pounds of
apples, you will ask for **un kilo et demi de pommes.**

● To say you would like one kilo of apples or half a kilo of
grapes, just say:
Un kilo de pommes, s'il vous plaît.
Une livre de raisins, s'il vous plaît.

● Or you can also add before 'one kilo'
Je voudrais un kilo de . . .

● To say you would like five slices of ham:
Cinq tranches de jambon, s'il vous plaît.

● To express quantities: a bit more/less; a little:
**Un peu plus de . . ., un peu moins de . . ., juste un
petit peu de . . .**

● To say 'Like this', while indicating with your finger or
hand:
Comme ça.

ACTION
You're at the fruit market and want to buy some fruit.

Shopkeeper	**Qu'est-ce que vous désirez, Madame?**
You	**Un kilo de pommes s'il vous plaît.**
Shopkeeper	**Voilà.**
You	**Et je voudrais une livre de raisins, s'il vous plaît.**

You're at the supermarket at the butcher's counter. You
want to buy five slices of ham and some pâté.

A vegetable market.

Butcher	**Vous désirez, Monsieur?**
You	**Cinq tranches de jambon, s'il vous plaît.**
Butcher	**Voici.**
You	**Et un petit peu de pâté s'il vous plaît.**

The butcher shows you how much with his knife.

Butcher	**Comme ça?**
You	**Un peu moins . . . Comme ça! Merci.**

You go to the fish market hoping to buy some shrimps, but you end up buying two dozen oysters (**deux douzaines d'huîtres**).

You	**Est-ce que vous avez des crevettes, s'il vous plaît?**
Fishmonger	**Non, je suis désolée Monsieur. Pas aujourd'hui.**
You	(pointing to some oysters) **Ce sont des huîtres de la région?**
Fishmonger	**Non. Ce sont des huîtres de la région de Bordeaux. Elles sont très bonnes.**
You	**Alors deux douzaines, s'il vous plaît.**
Fishmonger	**Oui, bien sûr.**

REPLAY

1 If the word following **c'est** is in the plural, it changes to **ce sont**, as in **Ce sont des huîtres de la région.**

2 Here are more expressions to order quantities: **5 francs la pièce** (5 francs each); **25 francs la douzaine** (25 francs a dozen); **12 francs le litre de moules** (mussels are sold by the kilo or by the litre).

3 Expressing some/any. In French, use **du, de la** or **des** in front of the noun, depending whether it is masculine, feminine or plural respectively. **De l'** is used before words starting with a vowel or an h which is not pronounced.

Examples:

Je peux avoir —
- **du fromage** (masculine).
- **de l'eau** (before a noun starting with a vowel).
- **de la crème** (feminine).
- **des pommes** (plural).

Note that whereas in English some and any are not always used to express quantities, in French you always use **du, de la,** etc. For instance, 'There is water on the table' and **Il y a de l'eau sur la table.**

4 Expressing likes and dislikes. I like is **J'aime**, to which you can add **bien** (quite), **beaucoup** (a lot). I love is **J'adore** and I prefer is **Je préfère**. If you don't like something, say **Je n'aime pas beaucoup/du tout**. And if you really hate something, say **Je déteste.**

TRY OUT

1 You've been given a shopping list: two kilos of apples, one and a half pounds of grapes and six slices of ham. Start with 'I'd like'.

2 At the fish market, you ask for 200 grammes of shrimps and two dozen oysters.

3 You ask the fishmonger whether she's got some clams (**palourdes**). You're in luck. Ask how much they are. They are 45 francs a kilo. You will have half a pound. Build the dialogue between you and the fishmonger.

4 Say that you like mussels but you prefer shrimps. Add that you hate oysters.

QUIZ

1 *Pairs*. Can you match the quantities in the first column with the food items in the second?

A	**cinq kilos**	1	**d'huîtres**
B	**une livre**	2	**de jambon**
C	**une douzaine**	3	**de beurre**
D	**une tranche**	4	**de crevettes**
E	**cent grammes**	5	**de pommes**

2 *Some/Any*. Fill in the missing words, using **du, de la, de l'** or **des**. Choose either **je mange** or **je bois**.

café
bière
pommes
crevettes

3 *Anagrams*. Can you rearrange the letters to form the correct words?

a zinedoua
b racthen
c amegrm

WORTH KNOWING

You will find a baker in most villages. If there isn't one, you will find **un dépôt de pain** (a shop where bread is delivered every day). There's a wide variety of breads; here is a selection: **la baguette** (long stick); **la ficelle** (smaller and thinner than **la baguette**); **le pain**, also called **le parisien** (twice the size of a **baguette** but smaller in length). **Baguettes** also come in funny shapes such as **le pain épi** (**un épi** is an ear of corn). Rolls are called **petit pain** and come in different shapes. For those who prefer brown bread, you can ask for **un pain de campagne** (farmhouse bread), such as the famous **pain Poilâne** named after Monsieur Poilâne, the Parisian baker, **le pain complet** (wholemeal) or **le pain de seigle** (rye bread).

EATING A SNACK

WHEN IN FRANCE . . .

When you're eating out in France, you may want to go to
simple eating places such as **la crêperie** where you can
taste the traditional Breton **crêpes** (pancakes) and
galettes (savoury pancakes) with all sorts of fillings. In a
café, you'll find a selection of snacks. Look out for **Nos
sandwichs** (our sandwiches) with **pâté, jambon,
rillettes** (potted pork), **fromage** or **Nos délicieux
croque-monsieur** and **croque-madame** (toasted
sandwiches with ham and cheese, the latter with a fried
egg on top).

Here is a selection of snacks to help you along:

une galette au jambon, fromage (with ham and cheese)
une galette aux champignons (with mushrooms)
une crêpe à la confiture de fraise (with strawberry
jam)
un sandwich au jambon

ACTION

You are given a list of **crêpes** (pancakes) and **galettes**
(savoury pancakes). While you are looking through the
list, the waitress asks you whether you would like to
drink some sweet cider **(cidre doux).**

Waitress	**Vous voulez boire du cidre?**
Your wife	**Oui, une bouteille de cidre doux s'il vous plaît.**

Later on, you give your order.

Waitress	**Vous avez choisi?**
Your wife	**Une galette au jambon, s'il vous plaît.**
You	**Pour moi, une galette au jambon, fromage, s'il vous plaît.**
Waitress	**Et vous désirez des crêpes dessert?**
Your wife	**Oui, une crêpe au chocolat.**
You	**Et une crêpe à la confiture de fraise.**
Waitress	**Très bien. Merci.**

You are at the café. You order two halves of draught lager and ask whether they have sandwiches.

You	**Deux demis s'il vous plaît. Et vous avez des sandwichs?**
Waiter	**Oui, j'en ai au jambon, au pâté et au fromage.**
You	**Deux sandwichs au fromage, s'il vous plaît.**
Waiter	**D'accord.**

REPLAY

1 Ingredients and flavours are put last in French, usually after **au** (which is **à + le**), **à la** or **aux: un sandwich au jambon** (ham sandwich), **un pain aux raisins** (currant bun) and also **un café au lait** (coffee with milk), **une crêpe au sucre** (crêpe sprinkled with sugar).

2 You'll often hear the word **en**, as in **J'en ai**. The word **en** does not have any equivalent in English. It means some or any on their own. Look at these examples to see how it is used. **Vous avez du cidre? Oui j'en ai**, or **Vous avez des sandwichs? Non je n'en ai pas.**

3 When ordering an ice-cream, you will be asked **Quel parfum vous voulez?** (Which flavour would you like?).

4 Would you like anything else? **Vous voulez autre chose?** You may hear the waitress ask you this question. Your reply could be: **Non merci** or **Oui j'aimerais une autre crêpe/un autre sandwich**, for example.

TRY OUT

1 You and your friend are a bit peckish and thirsty, so you order a draught lager and a glass of sweet cider, along with two ham sandwiches.

2 You and your friend are going to a **crêperie**. You order two savoury pancakes (one with ham and cheese, the other one with cheese only) and a bottle of cider.

3 A bit later, the waitress comes and asks you whether you want anything else? What did she say? You ask for a vanilla ice-cream and a crêpe with sugar.

4 Finally, you ask for the bill and also for the toilets.

QUIZ

1 *Hidden words.* Try to unveil *SIX* food related words.

```
M H P S A V W D
L J A M B O N O
C T I W C·B C N
I R N U I S R P
G A L E T T E F
V C I D R E P E
J S E R O D E T
E V L I N P R D
```

2 *Fillings.* Can you fill in the missing words?

une crêpe - - - **confiture**
un sandwich - - **fromage**
une tarte - - - **abricots**

3 *What was the question?* Can you make the questions from the answers given?

Des oranges? – Oui, j'en ai.
Des galettes? – Non, je n'en veux pas.
De la bière – Oui, j'en bois.

4 *Letter Jam.* Find out what the order was by breaking this sentence.
Uneglaceauchocolatetunegaletteaufromage

WORTH KNOWING
The crêperie and the café are not the only places for a snack. Try a snack-bar for a hot-dog, or a fast-food for **un hamburger**. If you're on the beach, you'll often hear the sounds of someone shouting **beignets** (doughnuts) or **glaces**. It's quite common for vendors to walk along the beach selling their wares like this. If you're still hungry, who wouldn't be tempted by the array of tantalising cakes and pastries on display in the **pâtisserie** window? For simple fare, try **un chausson aux pommes** (apple-turnover) or **une religieuse** (choux puff filled with pastry cream).

EMERGENCIES

WHEN IN FRANCE . . .

With a few words and expressions, you'll be able to sort out most of your medical problems quite painlessly. If you visit the doctor you'll have to pay a fee. You'll also have to pay for the prescription. At night and at weekends, look for the **médecin de garde** (the doctor on duty) or **la pharmacie de garde** (the chemist on duty). You'll find this information on the door of the chemist, at the local police station (**commissariat de police**) and in the local press. In case of emergency, the number to ring is 17.

● To say that your foot hurts/that you've got a toothache:
J'ai mal au pied/aux dents.

● To say that you are ill:
Je suis malade.

● To ask somebody to call for the doctor:
Vous pouvez appeler le médecin/le docteur s'il vous plaît?

● A wasp sting/mosquito bite:
Une piqûre de guêpe/de moustique.

ACTION

Your wife has got a temperature (**de la fièvre**) and a terrible headache which worries you. You decide to ask your neighbour to call for the doctor.

You	**Bonjour Madame.**
Neighbour	**Bonjour. Vous allez bien?**
You	**Moi oui, mais ma femme est malade. Vous pouvez appeler le docteur s'il vous plaît?**
Neighbour	**Oui, bien sûr.**

Later on, the doctor arrives to see your wife. He thinks it must be a minor sunstroke.

Doctor	**Bonjour Madame. Ça ne va pas?**
Your wife	**Non.**
Doctor	**Où est-ce que vous avez mal?**

Lifeguard's office. Bain surveillé means bathing is supervised.

Your wife	**J'ai mal à la tête et j'ai de la fièvre.**
Doctor	**Vous êtes toute rouge. C'est une petite insolation.**

You've been stung by a wasp and you decide to go to the chemist's (**la pharmacie**) to get something (**quelque chose**) for it.

You	**Bonjour Monsieur. Je voudrais quelque chose pour les piqûres de guêpe.**
Chemist	**Oui. Voilà une crème.**
You	**Merci beaucoup Monsieur.**

57

REPLAY

1 A few useful expressions in case of emergency: It's an emergency (**C'est une urgence**); the doctor or the chemist on duty (**le médecin** or **la pharmacie de garde**); help (**au secours**).

2 To express your pain, start:

– either with **j'ai mal au/à l'/à la/aux** followed by the part of the body: **j'ai mal au dos** (back), **à l'estomac** (stomach), **à la main** (hand).

– or with **j'ai un mal de/d'** followed by the part of the body: **j'ai un mal de tête** (a headache), **j'ai un mal de dents** (a toothache).

3 Parts of the body. You can find a list on pages 80–1.

4 Position of the adjective. Adjectives are usually placed after the noun, but some like **grand** and **petit** go before the noun. Compare **une petite insolation** with **une bière française.**

TRY OUT

1 Tell the chemist that you have sunburn (**un coup de soleil**) on your back and that you would like a cream.

2 Tell your neighbour that your daughter is ill and ask her to call the doctor.

3 Tell the chemist that your head, your right arm and your left foot hurt. Ask him whether there is a doctor close by.

4 Tell the doctor that you're ill, you're cold and that you have a slight temperature.

QUIZ

1 *Missing consonants.* Find the missing consonants to understand the question.

a **Où e‑‑ ‑e ‑ue ‑ou‑ a‑e‑ ‑a‑?**

b **‑ou‑ a‑e‑ ‑a‑ au‑ ‑e‑‑‑?**

2 *Missing vowels.* Find the missing vowels to be able to understand the message.

a **J'‑‑ m‑l ‑ l‑ t‑t‑.**

b **V‑‑s p‑‑v‑z ‑pp‑l‑r l‑ d‑ct‑‑r?**

3 *Headache.* The different parts of the body have all been mixed up. Can you put them back in the right place? See pages 80–1 if you need help.

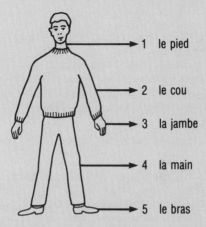

1 le pied

2 le cou

3 la jambe

4 la main

5 le bras

4 *Hypochondriac.* Can you find the missing words?

J'ai mal - - - tête.

J'ai mal - - bras.

J'ai mal - - pied.

J'ai mal - - 'oeil.

WORTH KNOWING
Medical matters
Before leaving for France, you must obtain the E111 form
from your local DSS office or from the overseas branch of
the DSS, depending upon the duration of your stay in
France. The E111 will enable you to get a partial refund
of your expenses. The doctor will give you a prescription
(**ordonnance**) if you need to get medicine from the
chemist's, and a form called a **feuille de maladie** (official
document the French forward to their Social Security).
You will need to stick on to the **feuille de maladie** the
vignettes which you will find on the medicine you're
prescribed. The **vignettes** are small detachable labels
which indicate the name of the medicine and its price.
You should send the **feuille de maladie**, once completed,
to the DSS on your return home to get the refund. The
refund will be between 70–80% of the total bill.

MEETING PEOPLE

WHEN IN FRANCE . . .
If you are invited to a party or a large French family reunion, you'll have to be able to ask people about what they do etc., and you'll be asked similar questions too. Here are a few expressions to help you along.

● To ask people what they do:
Qu'est-ce que vous faites?

● To tell people what your job is:
Je suis   cadre supérieur (a senior executive)
            à la retraite (retired)
            professeur (teacher)
(note that you just say **je suis** + your occupation)

● You can also start with 'I work in . . .':
Je travaille dans une agence de voyages (travel agency)
Je travaille dans l'édition (publishing)

● To ask people whether they are on holiday:
Vous êtes en vacances?

A family wedding.

ACTION

You've been invited to a party. This is one of the best opportunities to try out your French.

You	**Qu'est-ce que vous faites?**
Man	**Je suis professeur à Vannes. Et vous?**
You	**Je suis à la retraite.**
Man	**Vous êtes en vacances dans la région?**
You	**Oui. Nous avons loué un gîte.**

You're doing well. Now you meet a woman from the area.

You	**Vous êtes de la région?**
Woman	**Oui. J'habite à dix minutes d'ici. Et vous?**
You	**Je suis de Londres.**
Woman	**J'aime beaucoup Londres.**
You	**Qu'est-ce que vous faites?**
Woman	**Mon mari a une agence de voyages et je travaille avec lui.**
You	**Vous avez des enfants?**
Woman	**Oui j'en ai deux: un fils et une fille. Mon fils est marié et ma fille est à l'université.**

REPLAY

1 Have a look at Breaking the Ice (page 44) and Keeping Fit (page 68) to revise some useful expressions for socialising. The names of the members of the family are also worth knowing when meeting people. You'll find them on pages 81-2.

2 Yes is normally **Oui**, but it is **Si** after a question with a negative such as **Vous ne vous appelez pas Jane? Mais si, je m'appelle Jane.**

3 We've seen **en** in **unité** 11. Here is another use of **en**. If you end a sentence with a number, then make sure that you add **en** to the sentence like this:
Vous avez une voiture? Oui j'en ai une.
Vous avez des enfants? Oui j'en ai trois.
(Note also **Non je n'en ai pas.**)

4 If you want to know who somebody is, you can ask someone else **Qui est cette personne?**

TRY OUT

1 Say that you teach in Scotland, that you live in Glasgow and that you have two children.

2 Ask one of the guests at the party where she comes from, what her job is and whether she is on holiday.

3 Say that your husband is retired and that you haven't got any children.

4 You overhear a conversation on the train. A woman says that she lives in Spain **(Espagne)** but also has a house in Provence. She loves French cooking and is very fond of French wine. How did she say all this?

QUIZ

1 *Misinformation.* Somebody has got the wrong information about you. Correct them, starting with **Mais si.**

Vous n'avez pas de voiture?
Vous n'êtes pas professeur?
Vous n'avez pas d'enfants?

2 Can you finish off these sentences?

Vous avez des timbres?   (Yes I've got two)
Vous avez des enfants?   (Yes I've got four)
Vous avez une voiture?   (No I haven't)

3 *Human geography.* Where do they come from? Le Breton, l'Alsacien, le Bordelais, le Parisien, l'Auvergnat. Example: **Le Breton vient de Bretagne.**

WORTH KNOWING
Holidays and weekends
French people are entitled to five weeks' holiday per year. Most of them tend to take their holiday in the summer, with about 25% taking a second vacation in winter. Even so, only a small proportion of this figure actually go skiing, although the number has been increasing over the past decade. Many also go in search of the sun. The busiest period for the summer holiday is traditionally between the two bank holidays **(jours fériés)** of 14 July and 15 August.

Le week-end is important for the French. It is a time for the family, whether nuclear or extended, and also for the church to a lesser extent. The Sunday lunch at home or at a restaurant is a typical feature of **la fin de la semaine** (the end of the week). Large family reunions occur throughout the year. For those French people who have **une résidence secondaire** (second home) in the countryside or by the sea, the weekend may well be spent there.

BUYING POSTCARDS AND STAMPS

WHEN IN FRANCE . . .

The tobacconist's **(le bureau de tabac)** is easily recognisable by its red cigar-shaped sign, nicknamed **la carotte**, which is displayed outside the shop. You will often find the sign **Café-Tabac** or **Bar-Tabac** where you have the tobacconist and the café under the same roof.

● To ask how much it is to send a letter to England:
Pour envoyer une lettre en Angleterre, s'il vous plaît?

or

C'est combien pour envoyer une lettre en Angleterre, s'il vous plaît?

● To ask for two stamps:
Deux timbres, s'il vous plaît.

● A postcard:
Une carte postale.

ACTION

You've chosen ten postcards and you ask for ten stamps for England. The shopkeeper first asks you how many postcards you have.

Shopkeeper	**Vous avez combien de cartes?**
You	**Dix cartes.**
Shopkeeper	**Alors quinze francs.**
You	**Et c'est combien pour envoyer une carte en Angleterre?**
Man	**C'est deux francs vingt.**
You	**Alors, je voudrais dix timbres pour l'Angleterre, s'il vous plaît.**
Man	**Alors en tout trente-sept francs vingt.**

You go to the small **café-tabac** in a village to buy the regional daily ***Ouest-France*** and to have a small white coffee.

You	**Bonjour Madame. *Ouest-France* s'il vous plaît.**
Shopkeeper	**Voilà . . . quatre francs cinquante s'il vous plaît.**
You	**Et je voudrais un petit crème.**
Shopkeeper	**Oui bien sûr.**

REPLAY

1 To say a 2 franc 20 stamp, you have to reverse the word order and use **à** between them: **un timbre à deux francs vingt.** It is the same as **un menu à cinquante-cinq** or **une chambre à deux cent vingt-huit francs.**

2 To buy stamps you can of course go to the post office (**la poste** or **le bureau de poste**) which is recognisable by its yellow sign with the blue or white letters PTT. Inside you will see different signs above the counters (**guichet**). For stamps look for the sign which says **Affranchissements.** A letter-box is **une boîte aux lettres.**

3 The weather is always an easy ice-breaker when you meet people. You'll find plenty of expressions in your daily newspaper. Here are a few: **Il fait beau** (it's fine). **Il y a des nuages** (it's cloudy). **Il pleut** (it's raining). **Il y a du vent** (it's windy). **Il fait 25°** (it's 25°C).

TRY OUT

1 You ask the assistant in the **tabac** how much it is to send a postcard to Britain.

2 You and your friend go to the **café-tabac** to buy *Ouest-France* and to have a drink (two lager shandies). How would you say this starting with 'Can I have'?

3 Ask the assistant for twelve stamps for Britain. Ask him how much it is for the USA. He doesn't know. How does he say this?

QUIZ

1 *What was the question?* Can you translate the questions to complete this dialogue?
I'd like six stamps for Britain please.
Voilà six timbres.
How much is it?
Alors treize francs vingt.
Is there a letter-box nearby?
Il y en a une au bout de la rue à droite.

2 *Weatherspeak.* Can you be the weatherman?

3 *Location.* Can you finish off these sentences?
J'achète un timbre........(tobacconist's)
Je déjeune......................(pancake house)
J'habite...........................(Brittany)
Je bois un demi..............(café)

KEEPING FIT

WHEN IN FRANCE . . .

If you are a sports enthusiast, you may want to keep up your favourite sport while on holiday, or indeed try your hand at a new one such as **la pétanque** (French bowls).

● To say you play tennis:

Je joue au tennis.

● To say you take part in a sport (swimming, for example):

Je fais de la natation.

● To ask about hiring a windsurf board or a bicycle:

Je peux louer une planche à voile?
　　　　　　　une bicyclette/un vélo?

● For the day, half a day or for an hour:

Pour la journée, une demi-journée, pour une heure.

ACTION

You are on the beach and decide to hire a windsurf board (often referred to as **une planche** only). The woman asks you whether you can windsurf.

You	**Bonjour. Je peux louer une planche à voile?**
Woman	**Oui. Pour la journée?**
You	**Non, une demi-journée.**
Woman	**Est-ce que vous savez faire de la planche?**
You	**Un peu . . . Et c'est combien pour la demi-journée?**
Woman	**Cent vingt-cinq francs.**

You and your friend decide to book a tennis court for tomorrow morning.

You	**Je peux réserver un court de tennis s'il vous plaît?**
Woman	**Oui. A quelle heure?**
You	**Demain matin à dix heures.**
Woman	**Bon d'accord. C'est réservé.**

Windsurfing.

Bicycles for hire.

You and your friend want to hire bikes for the day.

You	**C'est combien pour louer un vélo?**
Man	**C'est vingt francs par heure.**
You	**Et pour la journée?**
Man	**C'est soixante francs.**
You	**Alors deux vélos pour la journée s'il vous plaît.**
Man	**Vous avez une carte d'identité s'il vous plaît?**
You	**J'ai mon passeport.**
Man	**Ça va. Merci.**

REPLAY

1 You've noticed **jouer** and **faire** before the name of sports. As a general rule, when you cannot use 'play' in English with the name of a sport you use **faire**, like **faire de la voile** (to sail), **faire du cheval** or **faire de l'équitation** (to horse-ride).

2 To say that you cannot play tennis or don't know how to windsurf, say **Je ne sais pas jouer au tennis** or **Je ne sais pas faire de la planche à voile.**

3 **Louer** means both to rent or to hire. You will see signs such as **Vélos à louer** or **Appartements à louer** (bikes for hire or flats to rent). You will also see signs saying **Location de vélos** or **Location d'appartements.**

TRY OUT

1 You want to hire two bicycles for the day. How would you ask? You also enquire about the cost.

2 A friend asks you whether you'd like to do some windsurfing. What does she say? Now tell her that you are sorry but you don't know how to windsurf.

3 You go to the municipal tennis courts in Vannes to book a court for 3 o'clock this afternoon. What do you say?

QUIZ

1 *A question of sports.* Using **Je joue** and/or **Je fais**, make up sentences from these drawings:

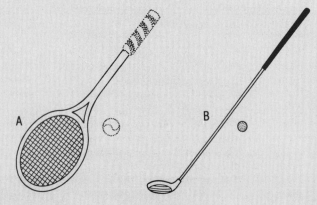

C   D

2 *Game, set and match.* Can you give the scores?
15–0; 30–15; 30–30; 40–30; deuce; advantage.

3 *Jumbled dialogue.* Can you put this dialogue into the right order?

a **Ce n'est pas possible.**
b **D'accord.**
c **Pour quelle heure?**
d **Je vous remercie.**
e **Pour 14h30.**
f **Je voudrais réserver un court de tennis.**
g **Alors 16h30.**

WORTH KNOWING

Les sentiers de grande randonnée (long-distance footpaths), known as **les GR**, offer not only a healthy way of spending your holiday, but also an opportunity to discover another side of France. They are indicated on the maps published by the IGN (**Institut géographique national**). These long distance walks are waymarked by two dashes (red and white) painted on the rocks or trees along the route. The super-fit may be tempted by the famous **Grande Traversée des Alpes**, a six-week hike.

If cycling is more to your liking, you will find a variety of landscapes suitable for the keen cyclist as well as the 'softy', from the easy pedalling of the Loire Valley or the Dordogne to the calf-stretching heights of the Pyrénées or the Alps.

A VERY BASIC GRAMMAR

This grammar aims at recapping and expanding on some of the points raised in the course of the **unités.**

CONTENTS

1 'A' and 'THE'

'A', 'an' and 'the' are called articles. In English, articles are often omitted before a noun, but this is much rarer in French. **J'aime les frites** (I like chips)

The word for 'a' or 'an' is **un** before a masculine word and **une** before a feminine word. With plural nouns, **un** and **une** become **des** (see also some/any below).
un homme; une jeune fille; des femmes

The word for 'the' is **le** before a masculine word and **la** before a feminine word. When words start with a vowel, or with some words beginning with 'h', this changes to **l'**. With plural nouns **le, la** and **l'** become **les**.
le café; la galette; l'orange; l'hôtel; les enfants; les gîtes

On the whole, there are no rules for knowing whether a word is masculine or feminine. You just have to learn them as you meet them.

Le combines with **de** and **à** as follows:
de+ le = du (**le prix du vin** – the price of the wine)
de+ les = des (**la fin des vacances** – the end of the holidays)
à + le = au (**je vais au marché** – I go to the market)
à + les = aux (**je vais aux Antilles** – I go to the West Indies)

2 SOME/ANY

'Some' or 'any', in phrases like 'some wine', 'some jam', 'some mushrooms', is **du, de la, de l'** or **des.** In English, note that some and any are often left out.
Je peux avoir de l'eau? (Can I have some water?)

Il y a du champagne dans le frigidaire (There is some champagne in the fridge). **Il y a de la crème?** (Is there any cream?) **Vous avez des amis en France?** (Have you got friends in France?)

'EN'

En means some or any on their own in sentences like:
Vous avez de l'eau minérale? (Have you got any mineral water?) **Oui j'en ai.** (Yes I have got some). **Vous avez des crevettes?** (Have you got any shrimps?) **Non je n'en ai pas.** (No I haven't got any).

En also means 'of it' or 'of them' in sentences like:
Vous avez des enfants? Oui, j'en ai cinq.
Vous avez des timbres? Oui, j'en ai un.
Vous avez des soeurs? Oui, j'en ai plusieurs.
Vous avez de l'argent? Non, je n'en ai pas beaucoup.

Note that **je + en** and **ne + en** change into **j'en** or **n'en.**

3 VERBS
In English, we say 'I live', 'you live' but 'he lives'. In French, the word ending changes more often:

J'habite	I live	**Je vais**	I go
Nous habitons	We live	**Nous allons**	We go
Vous habitez	You live	**Vous allez**	You go
Je suis	I am	**J'ai**	I have
Nous sommes	We are	**Nous avons**	We have
Vous êtes	You are	**Vous avez**	You have

To tell someone what you are going to do, say **je vais** and add the rest of your sentence.

L'année prochaine, je vais aller en Espagne (Next year, I'm going to go to Spain). **Demain, je vais acheter une voiture** (Tomorrow, I'm going to buy a car).

4 ASKING A QUESTION
There are various ways of asking questions:

a Make a statement and just raise the intonation at the end of the sentence:
Vous habitez en France? (Do you live in France?)
Vous allez bien? (Are you well?)

This also works with question words such as **quand** (when), **comment** (how), **où** (where), **combien de** (how much/many), **pourquoi** (why):
Vous partez quand? (When do you leave?) **C'est combien?** (How much is it?) **Vous avez combien d'enfants?** (How many children do you have?)

b Add **est-ce que** before the statement:
Est-ce que vous habitez en France? (Do you live in France?) **Est-ce que c'est loin?** (Is it far?)

If there is a question word, put it right at the beginning:
Où est-ce que vous habitez? (Where do you live?)
Quand est-ce que vous êtes en vacances? (When are you on holiday?) **Combien est-ce que vous avez d'enfants?** (How many children do you have?)

c Another way of asking questions is to change the word order. This is most common with **vous**.
Parlez-vous français? (Do you speak French?) **Où habitez-vous?** (Where do you live?) **Comment allez-vous?** (How are you?) **Avez-vous l'heure s'il vous plaît?** (Have you got the time please?)

To make a question starting with 'what' use **que**:
Using inversion (as above):
Que faites-vous? (What do you do? or What are you doing?)
Using **est-ce que** (as **b** above)
Qu'est-ce que vous mangez? (What are you eating?)

To ask a question starting with what is or which is, use **Quel(s)** or **Quelle(s)**:
Quel est votre numéro de chambre? (What is your room number?) **Quel est le train pour Strasbourg?** (Which is the train to Strasbourg?)

Note also:
A quelle heure part le train? (At what time does the train leave?) **Quelle heure est-il?** (What time is it?)

USEFUL WORDS

In this section, you'll find a list of additional words and phrases related to the 15 **unités**. (With words preceded by **l'** or **les**, the gender is indicated by an (m) for masculine or an (f) for feminine.)

UNITÉ 1

brandy	**l'eau-de-vie** (f)
chocolate (hot/cold)	**le chocolat (chaud/froid)**
coke	**le coca**
cold	**froid**
cup	**la tasse**
decaffeinated coffee	**le café décaféiné**
in a café, ask for	**un déca**

freshly squeezed lemon/ orange juice with water and sugar	**le citron pressé/ l'orange pressée** (f)
glass	**le verre**
hunger	**la faim**
I am hungry	**j'ai faim**
iced	**glacé**
juice (orange, apricot, apple)	**jus (d'orange, d'abricot, de pomme)**
refreshment	**le rafraîchissement**
shandy with lager	**le panaché**
sparkling mineral water	**l'eau gazeuse** (f)
still water	**l'eau non-gazeuse** (f)
strawberry flavoured milk shake	**le lait-fraise**
tea	**le thé**
tea on its own	**le thé nature**
tea with milk	**le thé au lait**
tea with lemon	**le thé au citron**

UNITÉ 2

breakdown	**la panne**
I've broken down	**je suis en panne**
car rental	**la location de voitures**
crossroad	**le carrefour**
headlight	**le phare**
indicator	**le clignotant**
jack	**le cric**
oil	**l'huile** (f)
to check the oil level	**vérifier le niveau d'huile**
parking	**le stationnement**
parking meter	**l'horodateur** (m)
puncture	**la crevaison**
route	**l'itinéraire** (m)
tyre	**le pneu**
tyre pressure	**la pression des pneus**
wheel	**la roue**
windscreen	**le pare-brise**

A few road signs

access for residents only	**sauf riverains**
give way	**vous n'avez pas la priorité**
headlights on	**allumez vos feux** or **phares**
all directions	**toutes directions**
other directions	**autres directions**
town centre	**le centre-ville**

UNITÉ 3

full	**complet**
room	**la salle, la pièce**
have you got any room?	**vous avez de la place?**
hotel-manager	**l'hôtelier** (m)
key	**la clé** (also spelt **la clef**)
luggage	**le bagage**
receptionist	**le/la réceptionniste;** **l'hôtesse d'accueil** (f)
toilets with washing facilities	**le cabinet de toilettes**

A few useful telephone phrases

who's speaking?	**qui est à l'appareil?**
hold the line	**conservez** or **ne quittez pas**
it's engaged	**c'est occupé**
there is no reply	**ça ne répond pas**
extension	**le poste**
code	**l'indicatif** (m)

UNITÉ 4

entrance free	**entrée libre** (f)
free	**gratuit**
guided tour	**la visite guidée**
left/right bank	**la rive gauche/droite**
pedestrian area	**le plateau piétonnier**

A few phrases

behind	**derrière**
between	**entre**
in front of	**en face de, devant**
it's free	**c'est gratuit**
it's five minutes on foot/by car	**c'est à cinq minutes à pied/en voiture**
you cross the bridge	**vous traversez le pont**
you go by the police-station	**vous passez à côté de la gendarmerie**
you go up to the station	**vous allez jusqu'à la gare**
you take the first street on the right	**vous prenez la première rue à droite**
you get off at Châtelet (tube station)	**vous descendez à Châtelet**

UNITÉ 5

blouse	**le chemisier**
cap	**la casquette**
dress	**la robe**
hat	**le chapeau**
jacket	**la veste**

mac(intosh)	l'imper(méable) (m)
pants, briefs	le slip
shirt	la chemise
shoe	la chaussure
sock	la chaussette
tie	la cravate
tights	les collants (m)
a pair of tights	la paire de collants

Men's clothes		Men's shirts		Women's clothes		Shoes	
GB	France	GB	France	GB	France	GB	France
34	44	14	36	8	34	1	33
36	46	14½	37	10	36	2	34
38	48	15	38	12	38	2½	35
40	50	15½	39	14	40	3	36
42	52	16	40	16	42	4	37
44	54	16½	41	18	44	5	38
46	56	17	42	20	46/48	6	39
48	58			22	50	7	40
50	60			24	52	7½	41
						8	42
						9	43
						9½	44
						10½	45

UNITÉ 6

cheese board	le plateau de fromage
cooked	cuit
plate of seafood	le plateau de fruits de mer
seafood	les crustacés (m)
fork	la fourchette
grilled	grillé; au grille
inn	l'auberge (f)
knife	le couteau
pepper	le poivre
plate	l'assiette (f)
rare (meat)	saignant
medium	à point (pour un steak)
raw	cru
salads	les crudités (f)
salt	le sel
spoon	la cuillère
teaspoon	la petite cuillère or la cuillère à café
well done	bien cuit (pour un steak)
wine list	la carte des vins

UNITÉ 7

arrivals	les arrivées (f)
departures	les départs (m)
dining-car	le wagon-restaurant
discount	la réduction
information	les renseignements (m)
journey	le trajet
left luggage	la consigne
lost property	les objets trouvés (m)
no-smoking compartment	le compartiment non-fumeurs
sleeper	le wagon-lit
the train from . . .	le train en provenance de . . .
the train to . . .	le train à destination de . . .
trip	le voyage
waiting-room	la salle d'attente

UNITÉ 8

attic	**le grenier**
bathroom	**la salle de bains**
bath	**la baignoire**
to have a bath	**prendre un bain**
bedroom	**la chambre**
basement	**le sous-sol**
cellar	**la cave**
central heating	**le chauffage central**
cupboard	**le placard**
current	**le courant**
dining-room	**la salle à manger**
drinking water	**l'eau potable** (f)
flush	**la chasse d'eau**
floor	**l'étage** (m)
garden	**le jardin**
guest bedroom	**la chambre d'amis**
hall	**l'entrée** (f)
junk room	**le débarras**
kitchen	**la cuisine**
lounge	**le salon**
room	**la pièce**
shower room	**la salle d'eau**

UNITÉ 9

America (American)	**Amérique (Américain/e)**
Austria (Austrian)	**Autriche (Autrichien/ne)**
Belgium (Belgium)	**Belgique (Belge)**
Holland (Dutch)	**Hollande** or **les Pays-Bas (Hollandais/e)**
England (English)	**Angleterre (Anglais/e)**
Scotland (Scottish)	**Ecosse (Ecossais/e)**
Wales (Welsh)	**Pays de Galles (Gallois/e)**
Ireland (Irish)	**Irlande (Irlandais/e)**
France (French)	**France (Français/e)**
Germany (German)	**Allemagne (Allemand/e)**
Greece (Greek)	**Grèce (Grec/que)**
Italy (Italian)	**Italie (Italien/ne)**
Spain (Spanish)	**Espagne (Espagnol/e)**
Switzerland (Swiss)	**Suisse (Suisse/sse)**

UNITÉ 10

anything else	**avec ceci** or **avec ça**
beef	**le boeuf**
butcher's	**la boucherie**
chicken	**le poulet**
cream	**la crème fraîche** (neither single nor double)
delicatessen	**la charcuterie**

frozen food	**les produits congelés** or **surgelés**
grocer's	**l'épicerie** (f)
lamb	**l'agneau** (m)
lamb chop	**la côtelette d'agneau**
margarine	**la margarine**
milk	**le lait**
full milk	**le lait entier**
semi-skimmed milk	**le lait demi-écrémé**
skimmed milk	**le lait écrémé**
mutton	**le mouton**
pork	**le porc**
potted pork	**les rillettes**
poultry	**la volaille**
take-away dishes	**les plats à emporter** (m)
tinned food	**les conserves** (f)
roast	**le rôti**
sausage	**la saucisse**
garlic sausage	**le saucisson à l'ail**
merguez sausage	**la merguez** (spicy sausage from North Africa)
smoked ham	**le jambon fumé**

UNITÉ 11

bun with currants	**le pain aux raisins**
cider	**le cidre**
dry	**sec**
medium dry	**demi-sec**
sweet	**doux**
pancake flambée with Grand Marnier	**la crêpe au Grand Marnier**
pancake sprinkled with sugar	**la crêpe au sucre**
savoury pancake with mushrooms	**la galette aux champignons**
savoury pancake with garlic and tomatoes	**la galette à la provençale**
toasted sandwich with ham and cheese	**le croque-monsieur**
toasted sandwich with ham, cheese and a fried egg on top	**le croque-madame**
sausage and chips	**la saucisse-frites**
waffle	**la gaufre**

UNITÉ 12

arm	**le bras**
chest	**la poitrine**
elbow	**le coude**

ear	l'oreille (f)
eye	l'oeil (m)
finger	le doigt
foot	le pied
hand	la main
head	la tête
knee	le genou
leg	la jambe
mouth	la bouche
neck	le cou
nose	le nez
shoulder	l'épaule (f)
toe	l'orteil (m)
tooth	la dent
thigh	la cuisse
thumb	le pouce
tummy	le ventre
I broke my arm, my leg	je me suis cassé le bras, la jambe
tablet	le comprimé
aspirin	l'aspirine (m)

UNITÉ 13
Occupations

banker	le banquier
consultant	le consultant
engineer	l'ingénieur (m)
executive	le cadre
foreman	le contremaître
freelance	freelance
I'm working freelance	je travaille pour moi
housewife	la femme au foyer
manager	directeur
nurse	l'infirmier (m); l'infirmière (f)
sales director	le directeur des ventes
sales representative	le représentant de commerce
secretary	le/la secrétaire
teacher (for children)	l'instituteur (m); l'institutrice (f)

Status

daughter	la fille
daughter-in-law	la belle-fille
divorced	divorcé(e)
father	le père
father-in-law	le beau-père
granddaughter	la petite fille
grandson	le petit-fils
husband	le mari; l'époux

married	marié(e)
mother	la mère
mother-in-law	la belle-mère
aunt	la tante
uncle	l'oncle
nephew	le neveu
niece	la nièce
son	le fils
son-in-law	le beau-fils
widow/widower	(je suis) veuve/veuf
wife	la femme; l'épouse

UNITÉ 14

envelope	l'enveloppe (f)
match	l'allumette (f)
matchbox	la boîte d'allumettes
newspaper	le journal
daily	le quotidien
weekly	l'hebdomadaire (m)
monthly	le mensuel
newspaper kiosk	le kiosque à journaux

UNITÉ 15

aerobics	l'aérobic (m)
angling	la pêche
gliding	le vol à voile
hang-gliding	le deltaplane
horse-riding	l'équitation (f)
mountaineering	l'alpinisme (m)
pelota	la pelote basque
sailing	la voile
skateboard	la planche à roulettes
skiing	le ski
alpine skiing	le ski alpin
country skiing	le ski de fond
water-skiing	le ski nautique
walking	la marche à pied

NUMBERS (les nombres (m))

0 **zéro**	
1 **un**	premier
2 **deux**	deuxième, second(e)
3 **trois**	troisième
4 **quatre**	quatrième
5 **cinq**	cinquième
6 **six**	sixième
7 **sept**	septième
8 **huit**	huitième
9 **neuf**	neuvième

10 dix	dixième	
11 onze	onzième	
12 douze	douzième	
13 treize	treizième	
14 quatorze	quatorzième	
15 quinze	quinzième	
16 seize	seizième	
17 dix-sept	dix-septième	
18 dix-huit	dix-huitième	
19 dix-neuf	dix-neuvième	
20 vingt	vingtième	
21 vingt-et-un	vingt-et-unième	
22 vingt-deux	vingt-deuxième	
23 vingt-trois	vingt-troisième	
30 trente	trentième	
31 trente-et-un	trente-et-unième	
32 trente-deux	trente-deuxième	
40 quarante	quarantième	
50 cinquante	cinquantième	
60 soixante	soixantième	
70 soixante-dix	soixante-dixième	
71 soixante-et-onze	soixante-et-onzième	
80 quatre-vingts	quatre-vingtième	
81 quatre-vingt-un	quatre-vingt-unième	
90 quatre-vingt-dix	quatre-vingt-dixième	
91 quatre-vingt-onze	quatre-vingt-onzième	
100 cent	centième	
200 deux cents	deux centième	
1000 mille	millième	
10 000 dix mille	dix millième	

1/2 un demi	1/5 un cinquième
1/3 un tiers	1/6 un sixième
1/4 un quart	

DATES (les dates (f))

The days of the week		**(Les jours** (m) **de la semaine)**	
Monday	**le lundi**	Friday	**le vendredi**
Tuesday	**le mardi**	Saturday	**le samedi**
Wednesday	**le mercredi**	Sunday	**le dimanche**
Thursday	**le jeudi**	On Sundays	**les dimanches**

The months of the year		**(Les mois** (m) **de l'année** (f))	
January	**janvier**	July	**juillet**
February	**février**	August	**août**
March	**mars**	September	**septembre**
April	**avril**	October	**octobre**
May	**mai**	November	**novembre**
June	**juin**	December	**décembre**

83

ANSWERS

UNITÉ 1

Try Out

1 Madame, s'il vous plaît *or* Excusez-moi Madame.
2 Deux cafés et un grand crème s'il vous plaît.
3 L'addition s'il vous plaît. Où sont les toilettes?
4 Qu'est-ce que vous avez choisi? *or* Vous avez choisi? *or* Qu'est-ce que vous voulez? Deux demis, un kir et un diabolo-menthe s'il vous plaît.

Quiz

1 C – E – D – B – A – F – H – G   2 A/3; B/4; C/1; D/2
3 C'est combien s'il vous plaît? Qu'est-ce que vous désirez? Je vous en prie.

UNITÉ 2

Try Out

1 Cent cinquante francs de super s'il vous plaît.
2 Le plein s'il vous plaît.
3 Vous pouvez répéter s'il vous plaît.
  Deux cent vingt francs.
4 Où est-ce que je peux trouver une station-service s'il vous plaît? Il y a de l'essence sans plomb?

Quiz

1 A Où est-ce que je peux trouver de l'essence sans plomb? A cinq cents mètres, à droite.
  B Où est-ce qu'il y a des toilettes? *or* Où est-ce que je peux trouver des toilettes? A quatre-vingts mètres, à gauche.
  C Où est-ce qu'il y a une station-service? *or* Où est-ce que je peux trouver une station-service? A quatre cents mètres, à droite.
2 Excusez-moi Monsieur.
  Où est-ce que je peux trouver une station-service s'il vous plaît? Vous pouvez répéter s'il vous plaît? Il y a de l'essence sans plomb? Merci beaucoup. Au revoir.
3 super, ordinaire, le plein.

UNITÉ 3

Try Out

1 J'ai une réservation. Je m'appelle . . .
2 Vous avez des chambres de libre s'il vous plaît?
  Je voudrais une chambre avec douche pour trois nuits.
3 Je voudrais réserver deux chambres. Une avec un grand lit et l'autre avec deux lits à une personne. C'est combien les chambres?

4 Est-ce que je peux téléphoner à Paris? Où est le téléphone?

Quiz

1 A/3; B/4; C/2; D/1.

2 trente-quatre francs; cent quatre-vingts francs; trois cent soixante francs; vingt-deux.

3 Bonjour – J'ai – Je m'appelle – Comment? – nuits? – pour – nuit – chambre – bains – hôtel – c'est

4 A/4; B/3; C/1; D/2.

UNITÉ 4

Try Out

1 Où est le quartier latin, s'il vous plaît?
C'est tout droit, puis la première rue à gauche et la deuxième à droite. C'est tout près d'ici.

2 Quelle heure est-il, s'il vous plaît? A quelle heure ouvre le musée?

3 Il est neuf heures et demie. Le musée ouvre à dix heures. Vous pouvez répéter, s'il vous plaît? C'est à 10 heures.

Quiz

1

un	premier	vingt	vingtième
quatre	quatrième	vingt-deux	vingt-deuxième
onze	onzième		

2 A Il est neuf heures.
B Il est six heures et quart *or* Il est six heures quinze.
C Il est midi cinq *or* Il est douze heures cinq.
D Il est minuit moins le quart *or* Il est vingt-trois heures quarante-cinq.

3 Pour aller aux Halles, vous tournez à droite au bout de la rue, puis la deuxième rue à droite et la première à gauche. Et c'est tout droit.

UNITÉ 5

Try Out

1 Je voudrais une jupe. Je fais du . . .

2 Est-ce que je peux essayer ce pantalon?
or Je peux essayer ce pantalon? Il est beaucoup trop long.

3 Le premier est trop petit et le deuxième est trop grand. Quelle est votre taille? Je fais du . . .

Quiz

1 Mon pantalon est un peu grand/un peu trop grand/
beaucoup trop grand/trop grand. Ma jupe est un peu
grande/un peu trop grande/trop grande/beaucoup trop
grande.

2 A Il est petit et gros   C Il est grand et gros
B Elle est grande et mince   D Elle est petite et mince

3 Je peux essayer cette jupe s'il vous plaît?

4 Je ne parle pas français.   Je ne suis pas anglais.
Ce n'est pas trop grand.   Je ne m'appelle pas Edward.

UNITÉ 6

Try Out

1 Une table pour deux s'il vous plaît.
Le menu gastronomique et une bouteille de vin rouge.

2 Je voudrais le plat du jour, et comme dessert une glace
et une bouteille d'eau minérale.

3 Monsieur s'il vous plaît *or* Excusez-moi Monsieur. Deux
cafés et l'addition.

4 Le menu à soixante-cinq et une bouteille de vin blanc
de pays.

Quiz

1 avez; plaît; menu; l'addition; eau minérale.

2 Vous avez choisi? Qu'est-ce que vous voulez comme
entrée/hors-d'oeuvre? Et comme boisson? *or* Qu'est-ce
que vous voulez comme boisson?

3 A/4; B/3; C/1; D/2.   4 A/3; B/1; C/2; D/5; E/4.

UNITÉ 7

Try Out

1 Deux aller-retours en seconde pour Lyon. C'est quel
quai?

2 A quelle heure part le prochain train s'il vous plaît? *or*
Le prochain train part à quelle heure s'il vous plaît? Et
à quelle heure il arrive? *or* Et il arrive à quelle heure?

3 Il y a un train à vingt-et-une heures quinze *or* à neuf
heures et quart *or* neuf heures quinze.

4 Pour aller à la Gare du Nord s'il vous plaît?
C'est la direction Porte de Clignancourt *or* Vous prenez
la direction Porte de Clignancourt.

Quiz

1 a le train circule tous les jours sauf les dimanches.
   b il part d'Angers à sept heures huit et arrive à
      Nantes à huit heures treize.
2 A Départs B Arrivées C Quai D Métro
3 Il est cinq heures huit *or* dix-sept heures huit.
   Il est onze heures quarante-sept *or* vingt-trois heures
   quarante-sept.
   Il est minuit vingt-quatre *or* zéro heure vingt-quatre.

UNITÉ 8

Try Out

1 Il y a trois chambres, un grand salon, une petite cuisine
   et un très grand jardin.
2 Voici la salle de bains. Voilà la cuisine. La voilà.
3 Pour ouvrir l'électricité et l'eau, s'il vous plaît, c'est où?
   or C'est où pour ouvrir l'électricité et l'eau s'il vous
   plaît?
4 Vous êtes dans un hôtel? *or* Vous êtes à l'hôtel? Nous
   avons un gîte. Pour combien de temps? Pour six
   semaines.

Quiz

1 Les voilà. Les voici. La voilà. Le voilà.
2 Oui, nous parlons français. Non, nous ne parlons pas
   français. Oui, nous habitons au Pays de Galles. Non,
   nous n'habitons pas au Pays de Galles. Oui, nous
   sommes écossais. Non, nous ne sommes pas écossais.
3 Je confirme la réservation du gîte pour un mois à
   Pézenas.

UNITÉ 9

Try Out

1 Je suis anglais, (je suis) de Londres, mais j'habite en
   Ecosse.
2 Comment t'appelles-tu? *or* Comment tu t'appelles? *or*
   Comment est-ce que tu t'appelles? *or* Tu t'appelles
   comment? Alternatively, say: Comment vous appelez-
   vous? *or* Comment est-ce que vous vous appelez? *or*
   Vous vous appelez comment? *or* Comment vous vous
   appelez?
3 Vous êtes d'où? Je suis de Madrid.
4 Je m'appelle … Je suis … J'habite à …

Quiz

1 m'appelle – J'habite – ne – pas – suis
2 E – C – B – F – A – D
3 FRANÇAIS   ANGLAIS   ECOSSAIS

UNITÉ 10

Try Out

1 Je voudrais *or* J'aimerais deux kilos de pommes, une livre et demie de raisins et six tranches de jambon.
2 Je voudrais deux cents grammes de crevettes et deux douzaines d'huîtres.
3 Vous avez des palourdes? Oui bien sûr. C'est combien le kilo? Quarante-cinq francs le kilo. Une demi-livre s'il vous plaît.
4 J'aime les moules mais je préfère les crevettes. Je déteste les huîtres.

Quiz

1 A/5; B/3; C/1; D/2; E/4.
2 du café; de la bière; des pommes; des crevettes.
3 a douzaine   b tranche   c gramme

UNITÉ 11

Try Out

1 Un demi, un verre de cidre doux et deux sandwichs au jambon s'il vous plaît.
2 Une galette au jambon, fromage et une galette au fromage. Et une bouteille de cidre.
3 Vous voulez autre chose? Une glace à la vanille et une crêpe au sucre.
4 L'addition s'il vous plaît Mademoiselle. Et où sont les toilettes?

Quiz

1
```
M H P S A V W D
L J A M B O N O
C T I W C B C N
I R N U I S R P
G A L E T T E F
V C I D R E P E
J S E R O D E T
E V L I N N P R
```

2 à la; au; aux

3 Vous avez des oranges? Vous voulez des galettes? Vous buvez de la bière?

4 Une glace au chocolat et une galette au fromage.

UNITÉ 12

Try Out

1 J'ai un coup de soleil sur le dos et je voudrais une crème.

2 Ma fille est malade. Vous pouvez appeler le médecin, s'il vous plaît?

3 J'ai mal à la tête, au bras droit et au pied gauche. Est-ce qu'il y a un médecin près d'ici?

4 Je suis malade. J'ai froid et j'ai un peu de fièvre.

Quiz

1 a Où est-ce que vous avez mal?
   b Vous avez mal aux dents?

2 a J'ai mal à la tête.
   b Vous pouvez appeler le docteur?

3 1 le cou 2 le bras 3 la main 4 la jambe 5 le pied

4 J'ai mal à la tête. J'ai mal au bras. J'ai mal au pied. J'ai mal à l'oeil.

UNITÉ 13

Try Out

1 Je suis professeur en Ecosse. J'habite à Glasgow et j'ai deux enfants.

2 Vous venez d'où? *or* D'où est-ce que vous venez? *or* D'où venez-vous?
   Qu'est-ce que vous faites? *or* Que faites-vous?
   Vous êtes en vacances?

3 Mon mari est à la retraite. Je n'ai pas d'enfants.

4 J'habite en Espagne. J'ai une maison en Provence. J'adore la cuisine française et j'aime beaucoup le vin français.

Quiz

1 Mais si j'ai une voiture. Mais si je suis professeur. Mais si j'ai des enfants.

2 Oui, j'en ai deux. Oui, j'en ai quatre. Non, je n'en ai pas.

3 L'Alsacien vient d'Alsace. Le Bordelais vient de Bordeaux. Le Parisien vient de Paris.
   L'Auvergnat vient d'Auvergne.

UNITÉ 14

Try Out

1 C'est combien pour envoyer une carte en Angleterre?
2 Est-ce que je peux avoir *or* Je peux avoir *Ouest-France* et deux panachés s'il vous plaît?
3 Je voudrais douze timbres pour l'Angleterre, s'il vous plaît. C'est combien pour le USA? Je ne sais pas.

Quiz

1 Je voudrais six timbres pour l'Angleterre, s'il vous plaît. C'est combien? Il y a une boîte aux lettres près d'ici?
2 Il pleut à Lyon. Il fait beau à Rennes. Il neige à Grenoble. Il y a des nuages à Strasbourg.
3 J'achète un timbre au café-tabac *or* bar-tabac. Je déjeune à la crêperie. J'habite en Bretagne. Je bois un demi au café.

UNITÉ 15

Try Out

1 Je voudrais louer deux vélos pour la journée, s'il vous plaît. C'est combien?
2 Vous voulez faire de la planche à voile? Je suis désolé, mais je ne sais pas faire de la planche à voile.
3 Je voudrais réserver un court pour 3 heures *or* 15 heures, s'il vous plaît.

Quiz

1 A Je joue au tennis *or* Je fais du tennis. B Je joue au golf *or* Je fais du golf. C Je joue aux boules. D Je fais de la voile.
2 quinze – zéro *or* à rien; trente – quinze; trente égalité; quarante – trente; égalité; avantage.
3 f; c; e; a; g; b; d.

FRENCH-ENGLISH VOCABULARY

(With words preceded by l' or les, the gender is indicated by an (m) for masculine and an (f) for feminine.)

d'abord first
l' **abricot** (m) apricot
d'accord ok
acheter to buy
l' **addition** (f) bill
aimer to like, to love
pour aller à to go to
l' **aller-simple** (m) single ticket
l' **aller-retour** (m) return ticket
alors so
l' **ami** (m) male friend; boyfriend
l' **amie** (f) female friend; girlfriend
anglais English
l' **Angleterre** (f) England
l' **appartement** (m) flat
appeler (le médecin) to call (for the doctor)
je m'appelle my name is/I'm called
arriver to arrive
avoir to have

le **bateau-mouche** river-boat
beau beautiful
beaucoup much; many; a lot
le **beignet** doughnut
la **bicyclette** bicycle
bien good; well
bien sûr of course
la **bière** beer
blanc white
bleu blue

boire to drink
la **boisson** drink
la **boîte aux lettres** letter box
bon good
au bout de at the end
la **bouteille** bottle
le **bras** arm
brut (cidre) dry (cider)

la **cabine téléphonique** telephone box
le **cadre supérieur** senior executive
le **café** coffee; café
le **café décaféine** or le **déca** decaffeinated coffee
la **carte postale** postcard
le **cassis** blackcurrant
ce/cette this
célibataire bachelor/ spinster
c'est/ce sont it is/ they are
la **chambre** bedroom
la **chambre d'hôte** B&B
les **champignons** mushrooms
changer to change
chaud warm; hot
le **chocolat** chocolate
choisir to choose
vous avez choisi? have you chosen?
le **cidre** cider
le **citron** lemon

la classe (première/ deuxième classe) class (first/second class)

la clé/clef key

combien? how much?
c'est combien? how much is it?
pour combien de temps for how long?

comme ça like this

comment how
comment allez-vous? how are you?

compris included

composter to validate

la confiture jam; preserve

la consigne left luggage office

à côté de next to; near

la couleur colour

le court de tennis tennis court

la crème cream

le crème coffee with milk

le croque-monsieur toasted ham and cheese sandwich

le croque-madame toasted ham and cheese sandwich with a fried egg

cru raw

la cuisine kitchen; cooking

cuit cooked
bien cuit well done

décider to choose
vous avez décidé? have you chosen?

le déjeuner lunch
déjeuner to lunch

le demi draught beer

la demi-journée half a day

demi-sec medium dry

le départ departure

désirer to like
vous désirez? what would you like?

je suis désolé I'm sorry

détester to hate

le diabolo-menthe lemonade with mint

le dîner dinner
dîner to have dinner

la douche shower

doux (cidre) sweet (cider)

la douzaine dozen

droite right

l' eau (minérale) (f) (mineral) water

écossais Scot; Scottish

l' Ecosse (f) Scotland

l' électricité (f) electricity

les enfants (m) children

l' entrée (f) starter

envoyer to send

essayer to try

l' essence ordinaire (f) 2-star petrol

l' essence sans plomb (f) unleaded petrol

l' **essence super** (f)
4-star petrol
être to be
vous êtes you are
excusez-moi
excuse-me

en face de in front of
faire to do
qu'est-ce que vous faites? what do you do?
je fais du tennis I play tennis
je fais le 19 44, puis mon numéro I dial 19 44, then my number
la **famille** family
la **femme** woman; wife
fermer to close; to shut
la **fille** girl; daughter
le **fils** son
français French
le **frère** brother
froid cold
le **fromage** cheese

la **galette** savoury pancake
gallois Welsh
le **gas-oil** diesel
gauche left
la **gaufre** waffle
le **gaz** gas
la **glace** ice-cream
grand tall; big
le **guichet** counter

l' **heure** (f) hour
quelle heure est-il? What time is it?
le **hors-d'oeuvre** starter

l' **huître** (f) oyster

ici here
il y a there is/are
irlandais Irish
l' **Irlande** (f) Ireland

le **jambon** ham
jouer play
la **journée** day
la **jupe** skirt

le **kir** white wine and blackcurrant

là-bas (over) there
le **lait** milk
la **lettre** letter
libre free
le **lit** bed
le grand lit double bed
le lit à une personne single bed
la **livre** half a kilo
la **location** for hire
louer to rent

la **maison** house; home
le **maillot de bain** swimming trunks/ costume
la **main** hand
j'ai mal aux dents I have toothache
j'ai mal aux pieds my feet hurt
malade ill; sick
marié married
le **matin** morning
le **médecin** doctor
le **menu gastronomique** gourmet's menu

merci beaucoup
thank you very much
moins less
le **mois** month
mon/ma/mes my
le **musée** museum

la **natation** swimming
noir black
le **nom** name
le **nuage** cloud
la **nuit** night
le **numéro** number

l' **oeuf** (m) egg
où where
ouvrir to open
**à quelle heure
ouvre?** at what time
opens?

le **pain** bread
le pain au chocolat
chocolate bun
le pain aux raisins
currant bun
la **palourde** clam
le **panaché** shandy
par ici this way
le **parfum** flavour
parler to speak
**vous parlez
français?** do you
speak French?
partir to leave
**à quelle heure part
le train?** at what
time does the train
leave?
le **pastis** aniseed spirit
le **Pays de Galles** Wales
le **péage** toll
le **pension complète**
full board

la **demi-pension**
half-board
petit small
le **petit déjeuner**
breakfast
peu little
un peu a little
le **pied** foot
la **piqûre de guêpe**
(wasp) sting
la **piqûre de moustique**
(mosquito) bite
la **planche à voile**
windsurf
le **plat du jour** the dish
of the day
plein full
le **plein (d'essence) s'il
vous plaît** fill it up
(with petrol) please
il **pleut** it rains
plus more
en plus extra
à point (viande)
medium done (meat)
la **pomme** apple
la **poste** (also **bureau de
poste**) post office
préférer to prefer
prendre to have
**qu'est-ce que vous
voulez prendre?**
what will you have?
près d'ici near here;
close by
la **pression** draught beer
je vous en prie my
pleasure
prochain next
puis then

le **quai** platform
quel/quelle which;
what

quelque chose
something

le raisin grape
la région area
remercier to thank
  je vous remercie
  thank you
la réservation
  reservation
réserver to reserve
la retraite retirement
  je suis à la retraite
  I'm retired
la route à quatre voies
  dual carriageway
la rue street

saignant rare (meat)
salé salted
la salle de bains
  bathroom
le salon lounge
savoir to know; can
  je ne sais pas nager
  I can't swim
  je ne sais pas
  I don't know
s'il vous plaît please
la soeur sister
la sortie exit
la station-service
  petrol station
le sucre sugar
sucré sweet

la table table
la table d'hôte evening
  meal that you can
  take in a French B&B
la taille size; waist
le téléphone telephone
la tête head
le timbre stamp
tout all
  en tout all in all
  pas du tout not at
  all
  tout droit straight
  ahead
  tout de suite right
  away
  tout près d'ici very
  close by
le train à grande vitesse
  (TGV) high-speed
  train
la tranche slice
trop too; too much
trouver to find

les vacances holidays
la vanille vanilla
le vent wind
le vélo bike
vert green
le vin wine
  voici here is/are
  voilà there is/are
  votre yours
  vouloir to want
  vous voulez?
  do you want?

Other titles in the *When in . . .* series
When in Italy
When in Spain

Titles available in the BBC *Get by in . . .* series
Get by in Arabic
Get by in Chinese
Get by in French
Get by in German
Get by in Greek
Get by in Hindi Urdu
Get by in Italian
Get by in Japanese
Get by in Portuguese
Get by in Russian
Get by in Spanish
Get by in Turkish

Also shortly available
BBC French Phrase Book
BBC German Phrase Book
BBC Italian Phrase Book
BBC Spanish Phrase Book

BBC Books publish a wide range of language books and cassettes
to suit all levels. If you would like to receive a complete
catalogue of BBC language courses, please write to:
BBC Books Enquiries
Room A3116
Woodlands
80 Wood Lane
London W12 0TT (or telephone 01-576 2587)